Unusual Uses for Ordinary Things

Unusual Uses for Ordinary Things

Instructables.com

Edited and Introduced by Wade Wilgus

Skyhorse Publishing

Skyhorse Publishing books may be purchased in bulk at special discounts for sales promotion, corporate gifts, fund-raising, or educational purposes. Special editions can also be created to specifications. For details, contact the Special Sales Department, Skyhorse Publishing, 307 West 36th Street, 11th Floor, New York, NY 10018 or info@skyhorsepublishing.com.

Skyhorse® and Skyhorse Publishing® are registered trademarks of Skyhorse Publishing, Inc.®, a Delaware corporation.

www.skyhorsepublishing.com

10 9 8 7 6 5 4 3 2

Library of Congress Cataloging-in-Publication Data

Unusual uses for ordinary things / Instructables.com ; edited and introduced by Wade Wilgus.
     pages cm
 ISBN 978-1-62087-725-8
 1. Inventions--Popular works.   I. Wilgus, Wade, editor. II. Instructables (Firm)
 T47.U58 2013
 600--dc23

                2012044008

Printed in China

Table of Contents

Introduction

Your house is full of hidden treasures, everyday items with the potential to be so much more. In this collection of twenty-five Instructables, you will learn unusual ways to use mundane items such as tennis balls, cheap vodka, nail polish, tea bags, coffee grounds, and medicated chest rub. From using the cheap vodka as a window cleaner to chucking a couple tennis balls into the dryer to fluff up your towels, we've got the advice to help you save money, save time, and make the most of what you've got. Let us help you use your stuff. Unusually.

Wherever possible, we investigated the unusual applications of these items ourselves. In doing our research, we discovered many potential uses that were more hopeful than helpful. Each of these Instructables was composed by an Instructables editor, and the uses described herein actually work. We smeared mayonnaise and baby oil on things, stuffed pantyhose in places where pantyhose really don't belong, and tested many uses that just didn't make the cut.

What Is Instructables?

Instructables is the most popular project-sharing community on the Internet. We provide easy publishing tools to enable passionate, creative people like you to share their most innovative projects, recipes, skills, and ideas. Instructables has over 40,000 projects covering all subjects, including crafts, art, electronics, kids, home improvement, pets, outdoors, reuse, bikes, cars, robotics, food, decorating, woodworking, costuming, games, and more. Check it out today!

* Special thanks to Instructables Interactive Designer Gary Lu for the Instructables Robot illustrations!

Section 1
From the Refrigerator

10 Unusual Uses for Butter

By Karen Howard
(http://www.instructables.com/id/10-Unusual-Uses-for-Butter/)

De-Sticks

Around the House

Tough Pill to Swallow

Beautify

Cat Training

Prolongs Shelf Life

Don't Boil Over

Ring Removal

Something Fishy

If all else fails . . .

Not only can you smear butter on your food, but it has some great uses around your home. This just goes to show that butter goes well with everything.

So grab that stick, and let's go make Paula Deen proud!

Use 1: De-Sticks

The natural oils in butter are perfect for combating anything and everything sticky. If you've been crafting and got some glue on your hands, rub them with butter before washing with soap and water.

After your in-home wax treatment, your legs are hair-free but still have some waxy remnants. Just like with the glue, rub a bit of butter on it, and the whole mess will wash off with soap and water.

Gum in your hair? Never fear! Apply softened butter to your locks, and the bubble gum will glide off pain-free.

Maybe you parked your car under an especially sappy tree, or perhaps you got a bit over-enthusiastic while tree-hugging. If you've got sap all over, dislodge it by rubbing some soft butter on the spot with a cloth. Wipe away and wash with soap and water.

If you need to cut up some sticky food (pies, dates, toffee, marshmallows, etc.) spread a knife very thinly with butter before slicing in. It will slide through easily without sticking—and add a few more delicious calories to your plate.

Use 2: Around the House

If you're out of WD-40 or don't have any oil, you can stop a door from squeaking by rubbing a little butter on the hinge.

To shine up cast iron, a small dab of butter on a cotton rag will make your metal look like new. This works well with other metals as well.

Butter can also be used to add shine to your leather baseball gloves, jackets, belts, wallets, purses, etc. Because butter contains proteins, it has plenty of amino acids and won't hurt the leather. Simply rub a small amount of butter on your leather goods for a nice shine.

Use 3: Tough Pill to Swallow

Some people swear a spoon full of sugar does the trick—but if you're swallowing down horse pills, you need something more substantial. Pills covered with a light layer of butter will help the medicine go down.

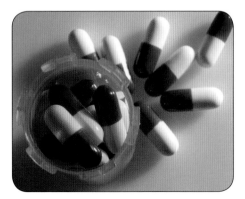

Use 4: Beautify

These same proteins that are good for your leather are good for your own skin, too! Rub a small amount of butter around your hands or other dry/damaged areas of skin. Rinse off with mild soap and water, and you'll feel the difference. Butter also keeps cuticles soft and flexible and fingernails less brittle.

Butter is excellent for treating skin irritations like nasty rashes. Rub a generous amount of butter on these irritations twice a day. Allow it to air for an hour or so each day. Cover with a bandage after applying the second daily coating of butter, and within a few days, the wound should be gone.

If you run out of shaving cream and need smooth skin in a pinch, use a knob of butter on wet skin and get a nice, close shave.

Butter can also be an excellent substitute for hair conditioners. It provides essential amino acids to fine, limp hair. Comb a little butter through your hair after you use your regular shampoo. Rinse the butter with moderately warm water for a shiny, healthy head of hair. Take that, Pantene Pro-V!

Use 5: Cat Training

Hey cat people—next time you move, butter your cat's paws before you let him outdoors for the first time at your new residence. Instead of darting out the door in a panic, the cat will sit down to lick the butter, which gives your furry friend a little time to become aware of his surroundings. Not only is butter a tasty treat, but your cat's coat will be glossier and the grease from the butter will keep fur balls at bay.

Use 6: Prolongs Shelf Life

Leftovers? Butter can help. If you're worried about how long your hard cheeses will last, apply a light coat of butter to keep them fresh and free of mold. Each time you use the cheese, coat the cut edge with butter before you re-wrap it and put it back in the fridge. This trick also works well for onions. Rub butter on the cut surface and wrap the leftover onion in aluminum foil before refrigerating it.

Use 7: Don't Boil Over

Stop pasta water from boiling over by adding a knob of butter to the water when boiling.

Use 8: Ring Removal

Ever tried on a small ring and experienced that moment of panic when you can't get it off? Next time that happens, remove the ring by gently rubbing a little butter around your finger joint and easing the ring off. You may have to do it a few times until it slides off.

Use 9: Something Fishy

Sure, your fishing trip was a big success, but now your hands reek of fish. Rub some butter on your hands, wash with warm water and soap, and everything will smell clean and fresh again.

Use 10: If all else fails . . .

. . . and you're left with an obscene amount of butter, go ahead and carve a sculpture. Or experiment with a deep-fryer.

6 Unusual Uses for Eggs

By Karen Howard

(http://www.instructables.com/id/6-Unusual-Uses-for-Eggs/)

Eggsotic Beauty Product

Eggceptional Glue

Eggstraordinary for Plants

Eggsactly like a First-Aid Kit

Eggcellent Cleaning Product

Eggstra Beautiful Jewelry

You know something's good when it's sold in packages of twelve. Eggs are incredibly versatile. This is my ode to those slimy insides that make breakfast worth waking up for. (Get ready for some pretty egg-splosive puns.)

Use 1: Eggsotic Beauty Product

If your hair has been lacking that extra something-something lately, worry no more! You don't have to shell out the major bucks; merely break a few eggshells instead! Eggs are rich in proteins that are very similar to those found in our hair, so they make great conditioning and strengthening masks. Try beating an egg (or a couple yolks if your hair is especially dry) with a bit of olive oil, and apply to your hair once frothy. If you want to smell less like an omelet, and more like you've just come home from the salon, add a couple drops of a scented oil. Leave on for about 20 minutes, and then rinse with warm water.

Fun tip: If Fido's coat has also been lacking luster, add a scrambled egg to his food every week. Your pets will love this tasty treat, and they'll be turning heads at the dog park in no time. As always, raw eggs are off limits, because they could be contaminated with salmonella.

Let's move this eggy beauty regimen south of the hairline to your face. Egg yolks and whites both have valuable qualities on their own for your skin, so there are a couple different facial treatments you can do with eggs.

With egg whites, you can make a soothing anti-aging cleanser that smoothes the skin. Whisk whites with a little bit of water and wash over your face. After rinsing off, you should find puffiness diminished and your pores looking smaller.

Egg yolks are very rich in Vitamin A, which is great for moisturizing. Just as you did with the whites, whisk these yolks with some water and use to wash your face.

If you have a large supply of eggs, perhaps a chicken coop all your own, alternate between these cleansers each night for best results.

Use 2: Eggceptional Glue

If you are out in the barn making crafts and happen to run out of glue, fear no more! Simply walk over to the hen house and grab an egg.

Egg whites are pretty sticky as they dry, and can easily double as an Elmer's substitute when gluing paper or light cardboard. You can also use egg whites instead of glue in your papier-mâché project by mixing them with flour, water, sugar, and some alum.

Use 3: Eggstraordinary for Plants

Are you eating a hardboiled egg right now? Wait! Don't pour out the water you used to boil it just yet!

Eggshells contain a high amount of calcium, which plants love. Let your hard-boiled-egg water cool, and use it to water your plants. They'll thank you for it—especially your solanaceae garden plants (tomatoes, eggplants, peppers, etc.).

If you've broken a few eggs to make your French toast, be sure to compost those shells! Or, if you have a particularly straight break, consider saving the shells for seed starters. Rinse the shell halves out with warm water to remove the membrane. Poke a small hole in the bottom with a pin to allow for draining, and fill the shell with soil. Press in your seeds, which will draw in extra nutrients from the shell and grow up nice and tall!

Use 4: Eggsactly like a First-Aid Kit

If you're anything like me, you enjoy cooking but are rather clumsy in the kitchen. This does not pair well with sharp knives and hot pans.

Next time you're too enthusiastic cutting vegetables into a fricassee and cut your hand in the process, no worries! Hard boil an egg, and use that thin membrane between the white and the shell as a make-shift band aid. You can turn it into a thin kind of skin by applying enough pressure to stop the bleeding, and it also has scar-fighting nutrients. Plus, snack!

Or perhaps you bruised yourself when digging around the cupboards to find that spring-form pan or grapefruit spoon. Hard boil an egg, and (while it's still quite warm) peel off the shell and rub it on your bruise. The heat should dissipate some of the blood that's starting to collect. Plus, another snack!

Use 5: Eggcellent Cleaning Product

Remember how eggs are good for our own skin? Well they're good for cleaning leather, too! Egg whites' thick and sticky base easily removes dirt from your leather shoes. Or bag. Or wallet. Anything leather, really. Gently scrub the whites into your dirty leather, and wipe off with a damp cloth. The egg will also form a protective base covering on your leather, which gives it shine!

Use 6: Eggstra Beautiful Jewelry

If your silver jewelry needs some oxidation to bring out a design, break out the eggs! Eggs contain sulfur, which is the active ingredient in store-bought oxidation solutions. Note that this method of oxidation does not work on fine sterling .999 (but most commercially sold silver jewelry is sterling .925 or lower, so this shouldn't be too much of a problem).

First boil an egg or two, depending on the size of your jewelry. You only need the hardboiled yolk, so take a second to boost your energy by eating the cooked white. You all set? All right, let's continue.

Break up the yolks a bit, and place them at the bottom of a container that you can easily seal. Set a wire rack over the yolks so you can hold your jewelry above without directly touching the yolks. If you don't have a rack, use some paper towels. Place your jewelry in, and seal the container. Let sit for a day (or longer if you want it darker), and wash the silver with a bit of soap. Heads up: The yolks will smell pretty nasty after sitting out, so be sure to open your container in a well-ventilated area.

If you don't want the entire jewelry piece to be oxidized, use a buffing cloth to polish the areas you want shiny again.

9 Surprising Uses for Mustard (That Don't Involve a Sandwich)

By Karen Howard

(http://www.instructables.com/id/
9-Surprising-Uses-For-Mustard-that-dont-involve-/)

Oh mustard, how do I love thee? Let me count the ways . . . there's yellow, spicy, honey, Dijon, horseradish, whole grain . . . muscle relaxant?!

Yes, just when you thought your favorite condiment couldn't get any better, I present to you nine unusual uses for mustard that go beyond sandwich-making.

But first, a little mustard history!

Way back when, the Romans were first introduced to mustard seeds by the Egyptians. They mixed unfermented grape juice with ground mustard and called this concoction "must"—hence mustard!

Use 1: Soothes Sore Throats

Your favorite team just had their big game, and, after cheering them on, your throat is feeling a little raw. Hopefully you have some leftover mustard from that tailgate party on hand, because it will get you root-root-root-ing for the home team in no time.

Combine mustard, the juice of one half of a fresh lemon, one tablespoon of salt, one tablespoon of honey, and one half cup of boiling water. Mix the ingredients thoroughly. Let the mixture cool for 10 minutes. Take some in your mouth and gargle! Warning: This concoction will not taste or smell good. After a few rounds of gargling, your throat should be feeling a lot less sore.

For the truly adventurous and brave, put one cap of mouthwash into the mix before gargling. This will increase the nastiness of the taste, but will also heighten the benefits.

Use 2: Removes Unwanted Smells

They say to never judge a book by its cover, and the same usually goes for products. But I've been guilty of getting suckered into buying something based solely on the fact that the bottle or container it came in looked awesome. So when I've had my fill of said-product, but want to keep the container, what can I do? Simple—I rinse it out with some mustard and hot water, and I'm ready to start fresh.

Didn't see Pepé Le Pew on the road until it was too late? If you accidentally ran over a skunk and don't want to hold your breath every time you take a ride, it's time to get rid of that smell. Mix one cup of dry mustard into three gallons of hot water. Mix it well, and splash it onto the tires, wheels, and underbody of the car. Clean by spraying the solution off. Your passengers will thank you.

Use 3: Decongestant

Have you ever eaten something so spicy that you get sweaty, teary, and have to grab a tissue? Mustard's heat can be put to a good use here, and this kind of drippyness can be induced (in a controlled way, of course) to encourage decongestion.

In place of a topical decongestant, try rubbing some mustard on your chest. Place a cloth, damp with hot water, on top of the mustard. Within minutes, you will feel better. You will not only be able to smell again, but the first scent you'll be greeted with will be that of delicious mustard. Ah . . .

Use 4: Face Mask

Mustard, not only do you enhance the beautiful flavor of my food, but you also enhance the beauty of my skin. Awesome!

Need to look great for that big date, but all out of a traditional face mask? Simply spread a thin layer of mustard on your face. The milder, the better, so go for a classic yellow. Let mustard settle for a few minutes then rinse. After rinsing, your face will be smoother and will have a nice healthy glow—not to mention smell like a sandwich. Added bonus? If you use cucumbers on your eyes while masking, you'll be able to have a quick snack before you run out the door!

WARNING: Take a second before slathering up your face like a sandwich, and see if the mustard makes your sensitive skin react. Spread a little bit on your inner wrist. If you break out in some funky rash there, then I advise against putting mustard on your face.

Use 5: Relaxes Muscles

Work out too hard and now have some achy muscles? Mustard can help in a variety of ways, depending on the muscle pain.

If you're hurting all over, try a mustard-infused bath. Combine two tablespoons of mustard and one teaspoon of Epsom salts in your warm running bath water. Mustard will amplify the therapeutic effects of the salts, relieving you of muscle pains at a much faster rate than bathing with them alone. Leisurely soak in the bath for about 20 minutes to relieve minor muscle aches and pains. After your mustard bath, be sure to shower off to avoid the lingering scent of mustard on your skin. Unless you're into that, of course.

Feet exhausted from a long day of standing? Make a soothing mustard foot bath! Combine one tablespoon of mustard in a pan of warm to hot water. Stir the water well to completely dissolve the mustard, and dip those poor puppies in. This will leave your hands free to do more exciting things, like consume a sandwich.

Lower back pain? Pulled some strange muscle that you didn't know you had? End the agony by making a mustard paste for these targeted sore muscles. Combine powdered mustard seed and all purpose flour in a bowl (one part mustard seed to two parts flour) and slowly stir in warm water to make a paste. Spread the mixture on one side of a square of cheese cloth and fold. Now place the plaster on the ache, securing it with a bandage. Leave the plaster in place for no more than twenty to 30 minutes at a time and feel those aches and pains just float away.

Use 6: Beautify Your Garden

Bambi has been helping himself to your garden veggies a bit too much this season, and it's time to find a creative solution. Rub mustard on a tin pie plate and hang it on a post near your garden. One mustard-covered plate per corner will keep the critters out. Apparently the deer will mistake the scent of the mustard for the scent of sweaty farm workers.

Apparently, white mustard seed releases some nutrients onto the soil that can prevent the growth of weeds and other unwanted plants. Plant a handful of white mustard seeds near your prized roses, or simply scatter the seeds throughout your garden. Your weed count will significantly decline. Remember to do a bit of research before planting these seeds as some plants are harmed by mustard's secretions.

Use 7: Hair Conditioner

Mustard oil is a secret conditioner secret that salons don't want to get out. But here's the dish: Pour a generous amount of mustard oil (note: not French's) on your palm. Rub hands together, and then scrub and massage your hair. Once done, leave the mustard oil on your hair for about 8 hours, or for the entire day/night if you choose.

Before falling asleep, make sure you have a shower cap so you don't damage your pillows. Once time is up, rinse the oil with shampoo and conditioner. Upon rinsing, you hair will be softer and more bouncy, and you'll put those Herbal Essence commercials to shame.

Use 8: Burn Relief

Kudos to you for trying your hand at that crazy complicated recipe. But your over-enthusiasm got the best of you and you managed to get a serious burn. Whether it is a severe burn or a minor burn, it hurts like heck and the pain just won't go away.

Step 1: Put the burned body part under cool, running water. This will relieve some of the pain right away and will help to stop the progression of the burning.

Step 2: This is probably the best, and least known, remedy for throbbing pain from burns: ordinary mustard. There is something special (magic?) in everyday yellow mustard that quickly takes away the pain. Just spread a nice and thick layer of mustard over the area and go about your Iron Chef-ing. You'll find that the pain goes away almost immediately.

your clothes, no worries. There's a way to get out that stain.

Use 9: Other Interesting Uses

Mustard is also rumored to have some other extraordinary uses. If you get a chance, give these a whirl!

- Helps you catch fishing worms
- Temporarily fixes car radiators
- Makes a strong salivating powder (though if you're as much of a fan of mustard as I am, this one's probably implied)
- Makes a burger that much better

And, if you were a bit overzealous with your mustard and spilled a bit on

5 Great Lemon Tricks

By Gregg Horton (frenzy)

(http://www.instructables.com/id/5-Great-Lemon-Tricks/)

Invisible Ink

Mold Removal

Boost Laundry Detergent

Blonde Highlights

Electric Lemon

Usually used for making lemonade, lemons have many other non-food related uses. With a bag of lemons around the house, you can come up with some cool projects!

Here are five of the most interesting I found.

Use 1: Invisible Ink

You can make your own secret spy invisible ink with lemon juice. Take a Q-tip and soak it in lemon juice. Use the Q-tip to write on the paper. Once the lemon juice is dry, you can use heat from a lamp to reveal a secret message!

Use 2: Mold Removal

You can remove mold by rubbing lemon juice where you see it. Mold should dissipate soon after!

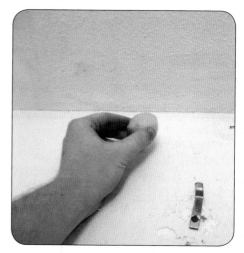

Use 3: Boost Laundry Detergent

Use one cup of lemon juice in your wash to boost the effectiveness of your laundry detergent.

Use 4: Blonde Highlights

Use lemon juice to get blond highlights. Just apply to hair and then sit outside. Repeat the process over a week's time for best results.

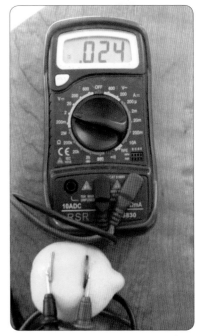

Use 5: Electric Lemon

Lemons can give you electricity!
1. Roll the lemon to get the juices.
2. Cut two slits in the lemon.
3. In one slit, place a dime; in the other, use a penny.
4. Now you have electricity from a lemon. You can test how much with a multimeter.

9 Unusual Uses for Mayonnaise

By Wade Wilgus (wilgubeast)
(http://www.instructables.com/id/
The-Mayo-Clinic-9-unusual-uses-for-mayonnaise/)

Polish Ivory Piano Keys

Condition Dry, Brittle Hair

Exfoliate Your Skin

Clean Up Crayon Marks

Strengthen Fingernails

Remove Tar, Sap, and Sticker Residue

Restore Wood Furniture

Remove Rings

Polish Houseplant Leaves

Mayonnaise, besides being a delicious French sauce from the 'naise family, has a number of uses beyond the kitchen. If you're caught without emollients or Goo-Gone, but have access to mayonnaise in individual packets (or a whole jar, if you're lucky), mayonnaise can save the day.

Containing the magnificently useful triumvirate of egg, lemon juice, and oil, mayonnaise is easily adaptable for a variety of uses from hair conditioning to removing bumper stickers.

Here are nine uses for mayo that will make your sandwiches insanely jealous.

Use 1: Polish Ivory Piano Keys

Your ivory piano keys are probably filthy. Such a shame, given that some poor elephant gave up his life for an afterlife of people playing "Chopsticks" on his teeth. If you're going to tickle the ivory, perhaps you should brighten it up a bit with some mayonnaise.

Just dab a little onto the dull key and leave it for 5 minutes or so. Then wipe off the mayo and buff with a different cloth until the ivory shines.

Use 2: Condition Dry, Brittle Hair

Mayonnaise has some delightfully emollient qualities. It'll soften and smooth hair for a sleek and chic look that can go straight from the runway to the kitchen.

Shampoo normally and towel dry.

Comb in at least a tablespoon of real mayonnaise (no need to go for the light stuff here, as very little will be absorbed through your scalp and deposited directly into your arteries), starting at the top of your head and working your way to the tips. Be sure to coat each strand of your luscious mane.

Leave it in for at least one hour. Try to stay inside while you wait because, you know, you'll have mayonnaise on your head and not everybody will understand it's amazing conditioning properties. To avoid staining all of your furniture, wrapping with plastic wrap couldn't hurt. Just don't wrap over your nose and mouth.

After your hour is up, wash your hair again using either a mild shampoo (like baby shampoo) or use a tiny amount of regular shampoo. It'll eliminate the fresh-out-of-a-French-bistro scent, but that's probably a good thing.

Style normally. Look extraordinary.

Use 3: Exfoliate Your Skin

Remember one step ago when we discussed mayo's emollient qualities? Well, it'll soften more than just hair. Got rough, dry patches of skin or elephant elbows? Mayonnaise to the rescue!

Apply a little mayo to problem areas like the elbows, knees, or your face. Leave it on for 10 to 15 minutes, then buff off with a damp towel or washcloth. Then use your normal moisturizer or lotion to lock in the freshness.

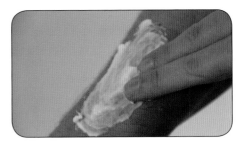

19

Use 4: Clean Up Crayon Marks

If you're not great at coloring inside of the lines, or you know someone under three feet tall who is into unintentional graffiti art, you may find yourself in need of some crayon cleanup.

Rub a little bit of mayo onto the crayon mark and let it sit for 5 to 10 minutes. Then watch it magically disappear when you wipe it away with a damp cloth.

Use 5: Strengthen Fingernails

There is jazzercise for cardiovascular health, spinning for aerobic exercise, and weight training for your biceps, but what about your nails? How can you improve your chalkboard attention-grabber without pulling nails out like a new hire in the gulags?

Try dipping your nails into a mayo bath. Soak your nails, cuticles, and the rest of your fingertips in some mayonnaise. Then rinse. Voila! Stronger nails. You'll be opening bottles and clamshell packaging bare-handed from now on.

Use 6: Remove Tar, Sap, and Sticker Residue

Now we venture further afield with our mayonnaise hacks. The car! Or bicycle. Or big wheel. Motorcycle. Hybrid Learjet. Whatever you've got parked on the street, under a tree, or in the garage, mayonnaise can take off whatever sticky, dirty mess you managed to get on your mode of transportation.

Cover the mess with some mayonnaise and let it sit for several minutes. Then wipe it off with a soft, vehicle-approved cloth. It may take a few tries for the tougher grime, but the lemon juice and oil combine to create a Goo-Gone equivalent that can be found for free in some delicatessens.

Use 7: Restore Wood Furniture

If your wooden furniture is covered in water rings, try to buff them out with some mayonnaise. Just like the crayon hack, leave a little mayo on the stain for 5 to 10 minutes, then buff out the stain. Try this on a surreptitious spot before you do it someplace conspicuous, or you may end up putting leg-warmers on your table or committing to a year's worth of seasonal placemats.

Use 8: Remove Rings

Mayonnaise will not only take the water rings off of your wooden furniture, it will also take rings off of your fingers.

The oil in the mayonnaise makes an excellent ring lubricant for those times when you must remove your ring but don't have any WD-40 on hand. Just work some mayo into the area around and underneath your ring, then slide the ring off. You may find that twisting helps, but stop if you feel any excruciating pain, numbness, or your finger falls off.

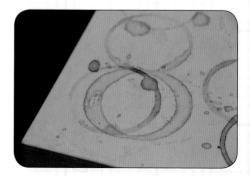

Use 9: Polish Houseplant Leaves

Growing up, my parents strove for parity in the household chores assigned to my sister and me. While I vacuumed the house, she would polish the leaves of our plants. Back then, I refused to believe that people actually polished their plants' leaves, but my mother assured me that it is a thing. And it is a thing that can be done with mayo.

Rub a little bit of mayo onto your matte and dull leaf. Buff it to a shine, then you'll have the shiniest ficus leaf in the world. Because leaf-shining isn't really a thing.

(Right? It's not a thing? I actually called my mom for more mayonnaise ideas, and this one was the second one she thought of. Second. She's either really committed to the lie, or this is real.)

Section 2
From the Kitchen

28 Unusual Uses for Aluminum Foil

By Wade Wilgus (wilgubeast)

(http://www.instructables.com/id/Thirty-Unusual-Uses-for-Aluminum-Foil/)

Use It in the Kitchen

Use It in the Garden

Use It for Cleaning

Use It for Laundry

Use It in the Garage

Use It with Technology

I love aluminum foil. It's recyclable, it's shiny, and it is super versatile. It can be used to clean, catch, protect, frighten, scrub, lift, soften, shape, grow, fix, sharpen, steam, attach, boost, and polish. We'll get into the specifics in just a moment, but first I would like to share a quick haiku about aluminum foil:

Aluminum[1] foil

The duct tape of the kitchen

All kinds of useful

Some of the following uses may surprise you. Some may anger you. Others may just leave you thinking, "I knooooow, I totally use it that way every day." Either way, these aluminum foil tips and tricks may just save your life. So settle in, grab a beverage, and position your roll of aluminum foil so you can gaze at it lovingly while I extol its many virtues.

---

[1] To those of you who speak British English, the syllabication doesn't quite work here. Aluminum was given an extra "i" to make it sound like all of the other -ium elements: helium, plutonium, uranium, etc. This is equally correct; I'm just going to use the lazy American dis-em-vowelled version. In the meantime, don't go getting any ideas about platinum. It'd sound weird with an extra "i." Say it aloud: "Platinium." That's how aluminium sounds in the colonies. Rich and vibrant and just a little bit vowelly.

Use 1: Use It in the Kitchen

Soften brown sugar

Brown sugar. It tastes so good. But it's not always the easiest sugar to work with because it gets clumpy and lumpy after a while. With some aluminum foil, however, you can soften brown sugar in the oven! Wrap your brick of brown sugar in aluminum foil, then pop it into the oven for 5 minutes at 300°F. Soon you will have softened brown sugar for all of your sugary needs. (You could always just do this in the microwave, but maybe you don't have any microwave- or oven-safe flatware . . . or a microwave.)

Pie crust protector

Some aluminum foil folded over the crust of a pie will keep the crust from browning and blackening and eventually falling off before the rest of the pie has cooked sufficiently. This use: useful but not unusual. Its usefulness far outweighs its ordinariness.

Pressure cooker lifter

Placing and lifting bowls into and out of a pressure cooker can be dangerous. Hot food, hot bowls, and slippery surfaces make for a situation fraught with danger. Aluminum foil makes an excellent lifting apparatus to safely and securely raise the precious contents of your pressure cooker without scalding your hands, arms, counter, floor, or curious dog. Just use a piece of aluminum foil that's the size of your bowl plus about eight additional inches. You're making a sling of sorts to lift out the bowl with your newly-made aluminum handles. Fold the foil lengthwise two or three times for strength, then place your bowl into the cooker with your shiny improvised lifter. Fold the handles down during cooking then use them to lift out your hot bit of deliciousness.

DIY cake pans

Oh no! It's your nephew's birthday and you were supposed to get him a cake shaped like Darth Vader wearing bunny ears. But you forgot because you were busy mayonnaising your hair. Don't panic! You can make yourself an awesome custom cake pan using aluminum foil and some creativity. Just use some aluminum foil inside another baking pan to create the outline of whatever cake you're trying to make. (This is great for county fairs when you want to make something in the shape of the county to woo city council into preferring your home-baked tribute to local government.)

Oven cleaner

You can protect your oven from thrills and spills by placing a few sections of aluminum foil beneath something that might bubble, bubble, toil, and trouble all over the floor of your oven. Don't foil the actual floor of the oven, as that could cause a build-up of heat to warp the bottom of your expensive appliance. Instead, lay some foil over the rack just beneath whatever it is that might erupt and create a mess. Instead of scrubbing until your elbows run out of grease, you can just ball up the soiled foil and recycle it. Bonus oven tip: To protect your heating elements from the harsh chemicals in store-bought oven cleaner, put some aluminum foil over them before spraying down the interior of your oven. This may cause a potentially explosive chemical reaction, but your heating elements will appreciate your thoughtfulness while the house burns down.

Scrubber

I'm a big fan of cast iron frying pans. They're great, but clean up is sometimes a disaster. Using salt and paper towels works most of the time, but egg and rice (and the combination thereof after fried rice) tend to grip the pan like limpets. With a little bit of crumpled aluminum foil, I can scrub off tough messes. This works anywhere you might find yourself scrubbing unusually hard like post-casserole Pyrex, forgot-about-the-pasta-and-all-the-water-boiled-off pots, and caramel that's Maillarded to the point of crumbly blackness.

Campsite cooking utensils

The next time you're camping, you can lug around an entire kitchen set, or you can take a light roll of aluminum foil and fashion your own utensils and pans. You can make a frying pan using a forked stick with aluminum foil stretched over the crook. You can easily make plates and bowls, wrap veggies and meat, or even fold a spoon, fork, or spork out of aluminum foil.

Reheat crispy things

I enjoy the occasional pizza delivered to my door from a company whose name comes from a popular dotted-tile game. But I can't always finish the pizza in one sitting, and I need to reheat the delicious cheesiness. I'll microwave when I'm in a rush, but if I want ideal flavor I go to the oven with some aluminum foil. I set the slice directly on the foil and fold an edge over the crust to protect it from the heat. Bake at 350°F for 5 or so minutes (or broil in high for two) and *bam*! Fresh-ish pizza. This method has the added advantage of instilling false olfactory hope in a roommate.

Use 2: Use It in the Garden

Scare birds

Some birds are scared of shiny things. If you dangle some aluminum foil from your fruit tree (especially with scary eyes drawn on), the more skittish marauders will move past your scrumptious feast, festooned with terror, in favor of someplace a little less dangerously delicious. Light-sensitive pests will stay away from your be-tinselled tree.

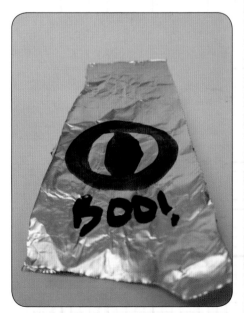

Protect saplings from deer and rodents

During the wintertime, the tender trunk bark of younger plants is a treat for starving animals. If you don't want Bambi to make it to spring, just wrap your trunks in aluminum foil for the winter. It should protect your shrubbery until the rosy-fingered dawn brings warmer and longer days later in the year. Don't leave it on while the plant is growing because it will need some room to grow.

Keep hungry slugs and bugs out

You work hard on your garden only to see the fruits of your labor devoured by God's creatures great and small. To keep the small ones from munching on your plants, make an aluminum foil mulch. Weed your bed, then lay normal weedblock over it. Place aluminum foil, shiny side down, over the weedblock to create a barrier that will send virus-spreading aphids elsewhere. (Reynolds also sells a special aluminum-treated paper for this purpose.)

Make a sun box

My apartment faces west, so the sad herbs in my balcony garden all reach out towards the setting sun instead of straight up. Rather than just rotate them every couple of days, I use a sun box (aluminum foil in a shoebox corner) to reflect the sun back into my plants. The box sits just behind the plants and is slightly less unsightly than a battery of cilantro aimed outward towards the San Francisco Bay.

Use 3: Use It for Cleaning

Ionizing cleanser for silverware

If I had any silverware that was actually made out of silver, I'm sure it would be tarnished. I just don't get the kinds of guests who merit the fancy stuff. But I might! So it's good to know that if I ever happen to own some tarnished silver, I could easily remove any oxidation residue with science! (And aluminum foil.) Just lay some foil down in a shallow, flat pan. Pour in some hot water and add a dash of salt and baking soda. Plop your silver items into your dish, making sure that they're touching one another and resting on the foil. Watch the tarnish disappear! If your silver is no longer recognizable as silver, wait about 5 minutes. After their bath, run some cool water over your silver sporks and foons and gently buff them dry with a soft towel. Soon you'll be able to impress everyone from the Pope to Lady Gaga with your shiny eating utensils.

Protect soap bottoms

I haven't used bar soap in forever. Not because I'm averse to washing, but because my soap dissolves into a damp, squishy mess before I get the chance to use it all up. But with a little bit of aluminum foil, I might be able to keep my bars of soap alive long enough to actually use them. To protect your bars of Ivory, just put a layer of aluminum foil on the bottom of your soap. It will protect your soap from melting slowly like the Wicked Witch of the West getting waterboarded at Guantanamo. And it looks nice next to a stainless steel basin. Very modern.

Slide furniture/protect feet and legs

Sliding furniture around on carpet is sometimes a pain. They sell special furniture-sliding disks for this purpose, but I don't want to buy something just to adjust my couch a few feet. Some aluminum foil on the bottom of the legs allows you to slide your davenport around cheaply and easily. You can use a little extra foil and make some furniture leg-warmer-style protectors when you're mopping or staining or setting your Roomba loose.

Use 4: Use It for Laundry
Destatic
I read somewhere once that using dryer sheets leaves a chemical layer on the things you use them with. For things like towels, this compromises absorbency. I like my towels to not stink after three showers, so I cut down on my detergent and switched from dryer sheets to balled up pieces of aluminum foil. I toss the foil ball into the dryer with my damp unmentionables, then let the magic of aluminum foil cure my laundry woes. (I also use a tennis ball to fluff things up and speed the drying time. I'm not sure it works, but it does mean I always have something to play with at the laundromat.)

Ironing speed
I learned to iron when I was a kid and had nothing to iron. Now that I have a closet full of Oxfords and other button-downs, I should be ironing. But I hate it. When I can't steal my girlfriend's hair straightener to fix the placket or collar, I use a layer of aluminum foil on the ironing board to speed up the process. The foil reflects the heat back into the shirt (as opposed to heating up the board itself), so the ironing takes just a little bit less of my life from me.

Attaching patches
My favorite pair of jeans ripped when I was in college. They fit wonderfully and looked great until I started clumsily jumping chain-link fences. Rather than throw them out, I thought I'd put in a nice patch for visual drama in the back pocket area of the pants. My plan was fool-proof: get an iron-on patch, then iron it on. And it worked! Too well. I ironed the patch over the hole, where it stuck very nicely. It also stuck to the inside of the pants, which was less nice.

When I tried to release my one-legged pants from their patchy prison, I ripped them beyond redemption. (I know, I should have reheated the patch before yanking on it. Hindsight. You know.) If I had used a small piece of aluminum foil in my pants to protect the insides, I could still be wearing those pants right now. Aluminum foil, where have you been all my life?

Clean your iron
Sure, my iron doesn't get enough use to get dirty, but it might. Someday. To get those unsightly chunks of melted plastic off of the nonstick sole plate (why'd you leave the iron on high on top of your buttons?), just run the iron on high over a piece of aluminum foil with some salt on top. The abrasion of the salt will help get the plastic off. Don't scrub the nonstick coating, though.

Steam silk and wool
Use the same technique as the speed ironing technique above. Put some aluminum foil on the ironing

board, then put your wild and woolly sweater on top. Use the steam setting on your iron and hold it a few inches away and ghost-iron your garment. The foil should reflect the heat back into the piece of clothing. Just make sure not to get too close or you will have to try the patching technique you just read about.

Use 5: Use It in the Garage

Sharpen scissors

There's nothing quite like the smooth, straight cut from a sharp pair of scissors. After a while, though, the cutting edge of your scissors may become dull. Rather than buy a new pair, why not just use a few pieces of aluminum foil to sharpen those shears? Just use your dull scissors to cut through 6-8 layers of aluminum foil. It won't make them Henckelsy, but it will improve the cutting edge.

Polish chrome

I have some chrome surfaces in my home. Escutcheons, especially. Because the chrome coating is contractor-grade thin, I've noticed some unsightly rusty pitting. To clean these off and restore their escutcheony luster, a little bit of aluminum foil and water will buff out those spots and make my bathroom look shiny and new. Rub until it looks good.

BBQ drip pan

Does your BBQ drip drops of sizzling fat and crusty chicken chunks? Do you not want to scrape and scrub the bottom of your grill every time you get a hankering for some smokey goodness? Put a layer of aluminum foil over the surface that you'd prefer not to clean. That's it. That's the tip. It'll prevent you having to get a special brush or expend any effort at all to clean up after grilling. Which is good, because that time should

be reserved for a food coma punctuated with the occasional meaty belch. (This tip also works for fireplaces.)

Clean the grill

You can use the leftover foil to scrub off the grill rack. It's remarkably satisfying when the foil shapes itself to scrape off a few rows of wire at a time. Not quite as effective as a grill brush, but it'll do in a pinch. . . . Say, when you're barbecuing at a public park and forgot your grilling utensils. Take nothing but pictures, leave nothing but footprints, guys.

Use 6: Use It with Technology

Wi-fi parabolic signal booster

Fold some foil into a parabolic dish to boost your wi-fi signal from your router. Sure, it's unsightly and kind of goofy, but sometimes you need to be able to watch videos of kittens falling down stairs when you're nearly out of wi-fi range.

Photography light reflector

Taking photos for my Instructables is always a chore. I hate that I have to wait for the light to be right at the office or at home, so I could really use one of those big light reflecting thingamajigs that real photographers use. With some aluminum foil layered over a piece of cardboard, properly-lit pictures are just a light source away.

Fix loose batteries

Sometimes the springs that hold batteries in place lose their springiness. With their springiness compromised, battery-powered devices might not work at all, or only work if you hold them in a certain position. (I'm looking at you, Comcast remote control that I had to hold vertically in order to DVR *Real Housewives of Albuquerque*.) With a folded up piece of aluminum foil, you can force those batteries back into place. Just fold up a little piece and wedge it into position so that the battery terminals line up correctly. This trick will blow the mind of a child whose Furby is acting up.

Protect your brain waves from eaves-dropping and mind control

Your thoughts are private. The government and super-advanced alien races (especially considering that they are probably in cahoots) shouldn't be able to read or control those thoughts. To combat telepathic control techniques that rely upon radio waves, you can fashion a protective helmet out of aluminum foil. Berkeley engineers have tested the wave-blocking power of aluminum foil and discovered that an aluminum foil deflector beanie actually magnifies extraneous signals beamed into a subject's head at certain frequencies. Probably propaganda.

4 Vinegar Mysteries Solved!

By Gregg Horton (frenzy)

(http://www.instructables.com/id/5-Vinegar-Mysteries-Solved/)

Polish Chrome

Cut Grease

Disinfect Cutting Boards

Drinking Vinegar for Health

Vinegar (acetic acid) is a sour liquid found in many homes. It has also been touted for centuries as a wonder drug and ultimate cleaning product.

But does it actually work? We will test five common vinegar theories here to find out.

Use 1: Polish Chrome

Our first theory is that vinegar polishes chrome fixtures.

Result: It works! It cleans it up nicely and doesn't leave a streak—hurray!

Use 2: Cut Grease

Next, a common conception is that vinegar is a good grease cutter.

Result: The grease, after being soaked in vinegar, came right off. I tried a bit of vinegar with some oil dropped in, and the oil broke down pretty well.

Use 3: Disinfect Cutting Boards

Some sources have suggested that cleaning a cutting board with vinegar will disinfect it.

Result: Inconclusive, because I can't see bacteria, but it cleaned off the stains on the board and left it looking cleaner.

Use 4: Drinking Vinegar for Health

I've read that drinking vinegar can help with muscle cramps and encourage weight loss. I figured I should try it out for myself.

Result: Vinegar tastes horrible (see picture 2).

Hope you enjoyed finding out how vinegar can help you solve more of life's problems!

5 Ways Baking Soda Can Help You Get a Date

By Gregg Horton (frenzy)
(http://www.instructables.com/id/
6-ways-Baking-Soda-can-help-you-get-a-date/)

De-Stink Your Feet

Brush Yo' Grill

Clean Your Sink

Put Out a Class-B Fire

Get Rid of Ants

Baking soda has a bunch of uses around the house. Some of you may be asking yourself, "Hey, Instructables, I need to get a date. How can I do this by just using baking soda?"

Here are five quick tips to help you get a date with the help of baking soda!

Use 1: De-Stink Your Feet

If your feet are like mine, they probably get sweaty and kind of gross after a day of running around. Prevent and solve the problem of stinky feet by putting some baking soda in your shoes. This will leave your shoes and feet smelling much fresher—perfect for getting dates!

Use 2: Brush Yo' Grill

Nobody likes kissing a nasty mouth. Put some baking soda on that brush and brush away to fresher breath!

Use 3: Clean Your Sink

Before you invite someone over to your house, you might want to do some clean up. Baking soda is great for cutting grease from that bacon marathon you had last week.

Use 4: Put Out a Class-B Fire

If you decide to impress your date by showing off your mad cooking skills, you might want to have some baking soda on hand to put out the grease fire you might start.

Use 5: Get Rid of Ants

Ants seem to not like it when you put a trail of baking soda in their path. Do this to prevent them from infesting your house and preventing you from getting dates.

I hope these quick tips help you get more dates than you could ever imagine!

11 Unusual Uses for Coffee

By Mike Warren (mikeasaurus)

(http://www.instructables.com/id/11-unusual-uses-for-coffee/)

In the Garden

Pet Repellant

Aromatic

Palate Cleanser

Fridge Deodorizer

Meat Rub

Fabric Dye/Wood Stain

Paint

Cleaning Abrasive

Facial Exfoliant/Faux Beard

Breath Freshener

Every coffee drinker knows the feeling they get when they have their morning ritual of a strong, hot cup of coffee. *Mmm*, just saying the word makes me smell it in the air. As a longtime coffee consumer and avid caffeine-scientist, I've seen my way around more than a few pots of potent, percolating brain juice. We all know the great benefits of coffee; it's:

- Hot
- Caffeinated
- Awesome

But did you know that coffee has a life outside of being a tasty bevvy? It's true! Coffee grounds can continue to be useful after you've had your morning fix and can work in some interesting ways. So, save those beans and find eleven unusual uses for coffee!

Use 1: In the Garden

Compost

Spent coffee grounds can be mixed with lye to make a great composting agent—you can even throw in the coffee filter, too! Worms in compost like to eat the bacterium that grows on the facets of coffee grounds. Though the grounds themselves are a food source, it also adds grit to the worms' digestive system, allowing them to digest better.

Fertilizer

Small amounts of coffee grounds can be added directly to top soil, especially on plants that like high acidity in the soil like azaleas or roses. Coffee is high in nitrogen, calcium, magnesium, potassium, and other trace minerals. Spreading around a thin layer of coffee grounds on your soil will allow a slow release of these minerals into your plants. Be aware of which plants like acidic soil (roses) and which plants don't (tomatoes).

Insect Repellant

Coffee has a very strong odor that many insects and animals do not like. In addition, it's been suggested that mosquitoes, ants, slugs, and maggots all dislike the acidity of coffee and will stay away from areas where there is a high concentration of acidic soil.

Use 2: Pet Repellant

Pesky neighbor's cat or dog always up in your flowerbed? Sprinkling coffee grounds, along with other powerful odor-emitting substances can keep those animals away. Most animals' sense of smell is much greater than ours, and, while coffee may smell great to us, it smells very unpleasant to a hyper-sensitive-olfactory feline. Used coffee grounds can be mixed with orange peels (or other citrus) and spread around flowerbeds for an inexpensive pet deterrent.

Use 3: Aromatic

Instructables member **noahw** made a coffee air freshener. "Enjoy that great coffee bean scent whenever and wher2ever you like." You can easily make your own with a pair of ladies stockings and fresh ground coffee. Simply double-up the stockings, fill with coffee grounds, and then tie off.

Use 4: Palate Cleanser

You may have noticed that many perfume counters at department stores have a small dish of coffee beans nearby (and if they don't have them, they should). These coffee beans are there to "cleanse your (olfactory) palate." The reason you want to smell coffee beans between perfume samples is that, when testing out powerful aromatics, it can get hard to discern one scent from another. The strong odor of coffee beans excites different areas in your olfactory, allowing a more sensitive sense of smell for the next perfume you want to sniff.

According to UC Berkeley scientist Noam Sobel: Smelling coffee aroma between perfume samples, as compared to smelling unscented air, actually works. The perceived odor intensity of the perfume from sample to sample stayed the same after smelling coffee aroma while it decreased when smelling air between samples. The pleasantness of the perfume, however, was similar after smelling coffee or air.   So grab those beans next time you're sampling perfumes or colognes and give your nose a break!

Use 5: Fridge Deodorizer

Borrowing **noahw**'s air freshener idea, I found that you can use coffee to help reduce refrigerator odors and food prep smells, like onions or other strong smelling food. Make a sachet of ground coffee and leave in the back of the fridge for a few days, the sachet should help absorb some of the strong food odors and emit a pleasant coffee aroma.

Use 6: Meat Rub

We all know coffee is great for breakfast, but what about dinner? Try a coffee rub on your next steak dinner for a unique flavor experience! I toasted fresh coffee grounds under a hot broiler for about 30 seconds, shaking often to prevent burning. The toasted coffee was then added with other steak spices, rubbed into the steak, and left to marinate for a few hours in the fridge. Cook steak as desired.

Use 7: Fabric Dye/Wood Stain

Coffee's dark color makes it a good choice for giving fabrics that "worn" look and wood an aged patina. You're not going to end up with a very dark dye or stain, but you will get a unique, weathered look. Depending on number of applications and type of material that the coffee is applied to, this method of dying and staining can produce some effective results.

Fabric Dye

Brew a regular pot of coffee and completely immerse the fabric of choice into the pot. You may need to place a small weight on top of the fabric to stop it from poking out of the coffee while it's soaking. Allow fabric to soak for 24 hours (or longer), then rinse the fabric and let it air dry. The result is a brownish, off-white color, giving the fabric an aged look. Try a few different strengths of coffee brews or lengths of dying time to achieve different shades.

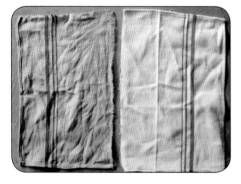

Wood Stain

Brew a strong pot of coffee and place the grounds back into the pot. Allow the coffee to cool slightly and then apply it to untreated wood. The coffee will stain the wood a slightly darker stain, but don't expect very dark results. Leaving the coffee grounds directly on the wood will result in a darker stain.

Use 8: Paint

Artists and crafters have used coffee and tea as a form of "paint" for ages. Regular brewed coffee can be brushed onto cardstock and will dry with a faded, brownish, textured look. With repeated applications you can build up your image and create depth. Make sure to take a sip between brush strokes.

Use 9: Cleaning Abrasive

Used coffee grounds can be used as a cleaning abrasive. Simply save up your coffee grounds and scoop some into your next dirty pot or pan before hand washing. The absorbent grounds are perfect for greasy pans and the small jagged edges of each ground helps in cleaning even the grossest of dishware.

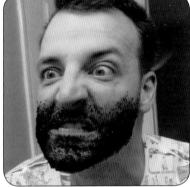

Use 10: Facial Exfoliant/Faux Beard

Facial Exfoliant

Coffee grounds are abrasive enough to scrub with, but are soft enough to be used on your face. Gently massage a small amount of spent coffee grounds into your face to use as an exfoliant. The sensation was like rubbing sand into my face and not unpleasant. My skin was left feeling smooth, tingly, and with an espresso aftershave aroma that would make Juan Valdez blush.

Faux Beard

Feel free to get carried away and give yourself a fearsome coffee-beard while you're doing the exfoliation.

Use 11: Breath Freshener

All out of mints? Sucking on a whole roasted coffee bean can work in a pinch. Just pop a whole bean in your mouth on the way out the door and you'll have fresher breath in no time!

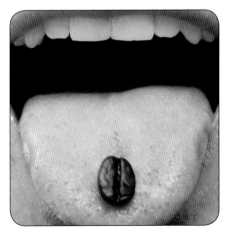

5 Ways Tea Could Help You Survive a Zombie Outbreak

By Gregg Horton (frenzy)
(http://www.instructables.com/id/
5-ways-tea-could-help-you-survive-a-zombie-outbrea/)

Soothe Tired Eyes

Stop Bleeding Gums

Stop Foot Odor

Soothe Injection Points

Reduce Razor Burn

Shotgun—check.

Machete—check.

Armored Personnel Carrier—check.

Twenty bags of tea—what?

When people think of "zombie outbreak," they never think to bring along some tea bags. Yet tea can come in very useful when the undead break out of Hell to ravage the land until we are all dead.

Here are five ways tea can help you survive the next zombie outbreak.

Use 1: Soothe Tired Eyes

After staying up all night fighting zombies, you'll need to freshen up your eyes. Put a wet tea bag on each eye for 20 minutes to freshen them up!

Use 2: Stop Bleeding Gums

Did that zombie punch you in the teeth again? If your gums are bleeding, you can press a tea bag onto the bleeding area to stop the bleeding and keep killing zombies.

Use 3: Stop Foot Odor

After the zombies take over, you'll be lucky to have one pair of shoes. Every day, to prevent foot rot, you should soak your feet in a tea bath to keep them healthy and fresh!

Use 4: Soothe Injection Points

You may need some inoculations after the apocalypse. If your shot area hurts too much, hold a tea bag there for 20 minutes to soothe the area.

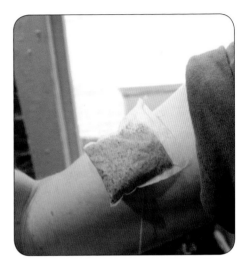

Use 5: Reduce Razor Burn

Supplies will be thin after the zombie apocalypse. If you decide to shave, razor burn is inevitable. Help cool down razor burn with a wet tea bag on the affected areas.

Good luck when the zombies take over, and remember to grab a carton of tea while you run for your life.

16 Unusual Uses for Cheap Vodka

By Sarah James (scoochmaroo)

(http://www.instructables.com/id/15-Unusual-Uses-for-Cheap-Vodka/)

Forget Expensive Dry Cleaning Bills

I Can See Clearly Now

Goo Be Gone

Mouthwash

Keep Flowers Fresh

Flakier Pie Crusts

Homemade Extracts

Window Cleaners' Best Kept Secret

Odor Eater

No More Flakes

Re-Usable Ice Pack

Hand-Sanitizer

Natural Astringent

Treat Wounds!

Drink It!

Infuse It!

Contrary to popular belief, cheap vodka is not only for boozehounds and college freshmen. There are many legitimate ways to use vodka that go beyond mere consumption: cleaning, baking, deodorizing, and even drinking (with a few tweaks for flavor).

Inexpensive vodka makes an excellent replacement for pricier products that do the same thing. Sure, a cabinet full of McCormick's vodka is more difficult to explain than some Windex. But the savings should make up for the worried looks and shaking heads you'll get for buying the cheap stuff by the case. At your intervention, you can teach them all these unusual uses for cheap vodka.

Use 1: Forget Expensive Dry Cleaning Bills

Spritz down your garments with a vodka dilution between dry cleaning to remove odors!

Unfortunately, this does nothing for stains, so once you've spilled red wine on your favorite white coat, you've really got no other option but to take it to the professionals. Or, you know, just soak the whole thing in red wine and make it new again!

Use 2: I Can See Clearly Now

A small spray bottle with vodka and water is the perfect solution for cleaning your glasses. Don't get ripped off by those greedy optometrists—make your own at home! One optical employee told me they make their own cleaning solution by combining water, alcohol, and a drop of dish soap. Give it a try! (May not be suitable for lenses with special coatings—try at your own risk.)

Use 3: Goo Be Gone

Vodka is a great solvent for sticky residue. Maybe you have a tiny spray bottle that used to hold overpriced lens-cleaning solution that you've decided to repurpose into a homemade lens-cleaning solution spray bottle, but it has sticky residue from the label that used to be on it. Problem solved!

Use 4: Mouthwash

Kill the germs that cause bad breath! Combine cheap vodka with a few drops of cinnamon, spearmint, or tea tree oil and let sit for two weeks. You've got your own high-octane mouthwash. Just make sure to spit after you rinse.

And next time you've had too much vodka, you can use the vodka mouthwash to freshen your breath! No one will be the wiser.

Use 5: Keep Flowers Fresh

Add a teaspoon each of vodka and sugar to water to keep freshly cut flowers looking great. The vodka kills the bacteria that would otherwise grow in the water, and the sugar provides nutrients the flowers need to thrive.

Use 6: Flakier Pie Crusts

Swapping ice cold vodka for water in pie crust recipes ensures a flakier crust. The liquid makes the dough more pliable to work with and then evaporates while baking, giving you a lighter result than water. Try this recipe for the perfect pie crust!

Use 7: Homemade Extracts

Vodka is a perfect base for flavored extracts, including chocolate and vanilla. Add vodka and flavoring to sanitized bottles and let it sit to develop flavor.

Use 8: Window Cleaners' Best Kept Secret

A vodka dilution makes a great window-cleaning solution. Combine vodka and water in a spray bottle and use newspapers for a perfect, streak-free finish!

Use 9: Odor Eater

Mist stinky shoes with vodka between wears to cut down on the smell. Feet can also be soaked in vodka to remove odors, as proven on *Mythbusters!*

Use 10: No More Flakes

A vodka rinse is a great solution for dandruff or dry scalp. Mix one cup of vodka with two teaspoons of rosemary and let sit for two days. Strain and use as a rinse to remove shampoo build-up or as a leave-in scalp treatment.

Use 11: Re-Usable Ice Pack

Combine equal parts vodka and water in a sealable freezer bag for a slushy ice pack to nurse injuries.

Use 12: Hand-Sanitizer

If you're someone who deals with germy kids all day, you know the importance of having hand sanitizer within arm's reach. Vodka is a natural enemy to bacteria, so reach for that small spray bottle and mist your hands generously. And if the kids are really giving you a hard time, no one will notice a few spritzes down the gullet, too.

Use 13: Natural Astringent

Dampen a cotton ball with vodka to use as a facial astringent to cleanse and tighten pores or dab onto cold sores to help dry them out.

Use 14: Treat Wounds!

Vodka acts both as a local anesthetic and a disinfectant, so it is perfect for treating open blisters and other minor wounds. It's even great for treating aching teeth!

Use 15: Drink It!

To enhance (remove) the flavor of cheap vodka, run it through a charcoal filter multiple times. The charcoal will get used up quickly, however, and if you're using brand-name filters, it may end up costing as much as a nicer bottle of vodka in the long run. Instead you should refill your charcoal filter at home!

Use 16: Infuse It!

If the filtered vodka doesn't do it for you, remember, vodka makes great infusions! Just add fruits, herbs, bacon, or skittles to round out your liquor cabinet with specialty, home-brewed, custom liqueurs.

Section 3
From the Bathroom

10 Uses for Your Old Toothbrush

By Carley Jacobson (Carleyy)

(http://www.instructables.com/id/10-Uses-for-Your-Old-Toothbrush/)

Remove Crayon Marks on the Walls

Brush Your Eyebrows

Clean Your Fingernails

Clean Your Shoe Soles

Remove Marks on Floors

Clean Grout Grime on Tiled Floors

Apply Hair Dye

Clean Appliances

Clean Hairbrush

Toothbrush Bracelet

TOOTHBRUSH

Here are some handy ways to re-use your old toothbrush. You may think this small little brush is only good for cleaning your teeth, but here are ten ways you can keep the toothbrush cycle going, including beauty and cleaning tips and tricks.

Use 1: Remove Crayon Marks on the Walls

Use shaving cream and a toothbrush to remove crayon marks on the wall. My landlord will never know I used my door as a canvas!

Use 2: Brush Your Eyebrows

Beauty and grooming tools can be expensive. I use this $1 toothbrush as an eyebrow brush.

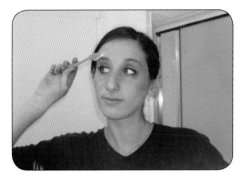

Use 3: Clean Your Fingernails

Brush that dirt out from under your fingernails. Just put a little soap and water on the brush and you're good to go. It feels nice on your nails, too!

Use 4: Clean Your Shoe Soles

When dirt and mud get stuck in the soles of your shoes, loosen them up with your toothbrush.

Use 5: Remove Marks on Floors

Use non-gel whitening toothpaste to remove stains from the floors and countertops.

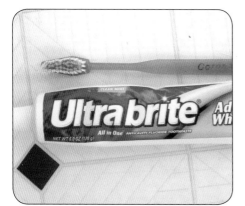

Use 6: Clean Grout Grime on Tiled Floors

Combine one part Borax, two parts baking soda, and two parts water to clear out that funky grime between tiles. Use this in the kitchen and bathroom.

Use 7: Apply Hair Dye

Apply hair dye yourself using a toothbrush. For quick touch-ups to gray hair or roots, apply mascara to a toothbrush—it will blend the color in your hair better than the mascara wand.

Use 9: Clean Hairbrush

Lift the hair out of your hair brush by pulling it up with your old toothbrush.

Use 8: Clean Appliances

Toasters. Microwaves. Coffee Machines. Use a toothbrush to clean off crumbs and stains that fall in those hard to reach spaces.

Use 10: Toothbrush Bracelet

Finally, when your toothbrush is at the end of the road, make a purdy toothbrush bracelet.

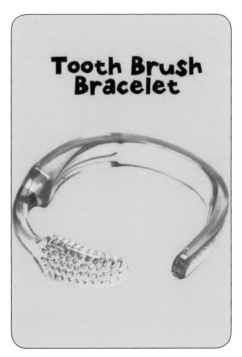

Tooth Brush Bracelet

9 Unusual Uses for Aspirin

By Wade Wilgus (wilgubeast)
(http://www.instructables.com/id/9-Unusual-Uses-for-Aspirin/)

Heart Attack Mitigation

Remove Sweat Stains

Restore Hair Color

Zap Zits and Punish Pimples

Treat Bug Bites and Stings

Organic Gardener's Dream

Treat Dandruff

Squeeze the Last Juice from
a Car Battery

Treat a Hangover

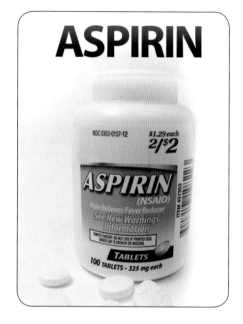

It's 6:30 in the morning and you feel a tightness in your chest. Antacids don't help. Your jaw is tightly set and your arm feels numb. Heart attack? Or is it an unreasonable response to a new zit? Either way, aspirin can help.

From heart attacks to zits, in the garden and the laundry room, aspirin has a ton of uses beyond relieving pain. Some of these I've tried, others I should try but haven't, and a few I hope to never try. You, the reader, are left to judge which is which.

Use 1: Heart Attack Mitigation

If you're feeling a bit of a heart attack coming on, pop some aspirin and dial 911. (Or your local emergency number.)

The aspirin has an anti-clotting effect that inhibits platelets from doing their little platelet-y jobs. You know, hanging out together in large groups, getting rowdy, and creating thromboses. This is perfect for those occasions when you're on the verge of death due to an unplanned cardiac episode.

According to the American Journal of Cardiology, chewing the aspirin has a more immediate effect than washing the pills down with a cool glass of water. So that's good to know. Especially if you're a man over 50 with less plaque on your teeth than in your arteries.

Use 2: Remove Sweat Stains

Sure, the collar of that undershirt looks fine, but the armpits are caked and yellow like you're developing uranium for a nascent nuclear weapons program. Gross. Apparently the aluminum salts in most antiperspirants mixes with sweat to create a mostly-waterproof stain. The salicylic acid in aspirin makes a nice little anti-yellowcake mixture that can eradicate those sweat stains.

Crush up enough pills and mix with water to create enough paste to cover the sweat stain of your choice. Let it sit for several minutes then rinse. Launder as usual. This treatment is good for any protein-based stain, so pull it out for those times when you get some of that nosebleed on your shirt or dribble egg yolk onto your pants due to over-over-easiness.

Note: Pound for pound, this is an expensive method of removing sweat stains (compared to using lemon juice, enzymatic meat tenderizer, or white vinegar), but it's a good thing to bear in mind if you're surprised by a serious stain in a random hotel room that stocks aspirin, but not meat tenderizer, in the lobby gift shop.

Use 3: Restore Hair Color

Big swimmer? Blond? If so, you know that chlorine can do a number on your hair. But a little aspirin can take care of that.

Dissolve 6–8 aspirin pills in water, then rub the solution into your hair. Let it sit for 10 minutes and rinse it out. The greenish effect should start to disappear after a couple of aspirin washes.

When I was in fifth grade, there was a girl in my class with hair so blonde and fine it looked like fiber optic wire. She was a swimming fiend, so her hair was always just a touch too green in the summertime. In middle school, she achieved the Edenic self-consciousness of Eve and began to use aspirin to fix the greenness. She is now incredibly successful and one of 17^2 female engineers in the whole world. Aspirin helped her become a foxy materials engineer—imagine what it could do for you.

Use 4: Zap Zits and Punish Pimples

Salicylic acid. It's one of the topical applications used for acne treatment, and it just so happens to be a natural part of aspirin.

Crush up the pill and add some water to make a paste. Apply the aspirin paste to your pimple and wait for several minutes. Rinse off without rubbing too much, and the pimple should diminish in redness and size. It's great spot treatment for those "haven't showered since Friday" weekend camping trips where you want to look your best.

Possibly true fact: The taste of salicylic acid can discourage bears from gnawing on your face.

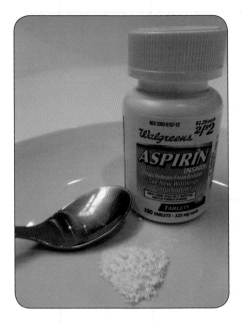

Use 5: Treat Bug Bites and Stings

Just like the acne treatment, a little dab of aspirin paste will do you when it comes to mosquitoes, flies, and other stinging and biting bugs out there.

A great little camping piece of know-how: Willow trees and their ilk contain the natural equivalent of Bayer. Some bark will have a similar effect to the paste described earlier. When I was a Boy Scout in Colorado, we used to strip small sections of bark off of aspen trees and treat the bug bites we brought upon ourselves by being fragrantly scrumptious.

Use 6: Organic Gardener's Dream

A crushed aspirin in water (one pill to one gallon) helps plants fight infection and stay alive during traumatic plant

---

[2] I know that there are more. But there are still too many girls being discouraged from careers in science and math.

experiences like transplanting, cutting, cloning, or zombie attacks. If your plants are dying in front of your eyes, it can be tempting to resort to extreme measures to rescue your little green friends with a water-soluble fertilizer. When stressed, however, plants can't really absorb all those delicious nitrates and phosphates. Dumping fertilizer on a dying plant is like giving a heart attack victim a multivitamin: not quite the ideal time for bio-availability. Aspirin is the solution (pun!) for your mild flora emergency.

According to the exhaustive research I just performed on Wikipedia, salicylic acid can induce specific changes in root, stem, and leaf structure that create more robust plants. It can also help fruits and vegetables grow bigger and stronger. It will help your plants resist disease, insects, and unusually weak hailstorms.

Additionally, an aspirin solution will also help your cut flowers last longer in the vase so you can go nearly a full week before raking up the dead petals. Unless you're playing the "he loves me, he loves me not" game, in which case you should just count the petals in advance to determine your romantic status and let the aspirin keep the bouquet pretty.

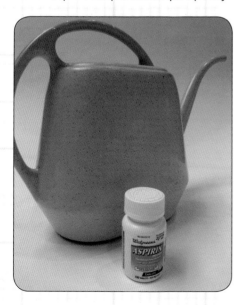

Use 7: Treat Dandruff

Itchy flakiness got your shoulders looking like snowdrifts? If you wear a black American Apparel hoodie that looks a bit like a heather gray American Apparel hoodie, perhaps you should consider using aspirin in your daily head-washing regimen.

Crush up two aspirins into the normal amount of shampoo you use, then leave it in for several minutes. Don't do it with a dandruff-specific shampoo, but this is a great method of maintaining great-smelling hair without distributing enough fine white powder to cause an asbestos scare or DEA raid. If you're concerned about wasting water while you wait, shut off the water and just hang out for a minute while the aspirin does its job.

Use 8: Squeeze the Last Juice from a Car Battery

Electrolytes. They're not just in sports drinks and the athletes who drink them. They're also an important part of a car battery. But sometimes your car battery needs an extra shot of juice to crank out just a little more energy to get your car moving. Aspirin apparently makes a lovely electrolytic stimulant that'll get you out of a really serious pickle. Because if you're popping open your car battery, things are probably pretty serious and AAA isn't coming any time soon.

Pry off the cover of the battery with a screwdriver or pry bar and drop two crushed aspirin into each cell of the battery. Theoretically, this should cause a chemical reaction that changes some of the sulfuric acid into acetic acid and provide just enough *oomph* to get the engine to start turning over.

For bonus MacGyver points, try using cola to take any corrosion off of the terminals. If it's really cold outside, heat up the battery with whatever you've got on hand. Pouring hot water over the engine and battery itself (with everything disconnected) might help. YMMV. Literally.

Use 9: Treat a Hangover

Acetaminophen + alcohol = vicious, liver-destroying poison. Don't take Tylenol when you've been drinking.

After a long night out on the town, if you are in any condition to do so, take two aspirin before bed. These will help decrease the severity of the hangover in the morning by inhibiting prostaglandins. (You know you don't want those prostaglandins running around inside of your body like evil elves while you have the spins.) Then take two more in the morning with some breakfast. It'll decrease the severity of the morning headache and decrease the elf- or prostaglandin-related swelling.

If it's one of those mornings where the hair of the dog sounds as appetizing as actual canine fur, aspirin's your ticket to a productive day.

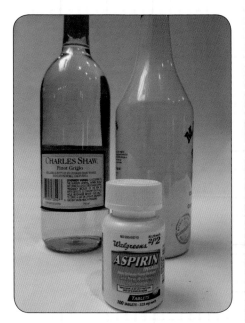

12 Unusual Uses for Baby Oil

By Wade Wilgus (wilgubeast)
(http://www.instructables.com/id/11-Unusual-Uses-for-Baby-Oil/)

But First, Some Don'ts

Get Latex Paint Off of Skin

Massage Oil

Remove Earwax

Take Off Eye Makeup

Bath Oil

Post-Shave Oil

Keep Warm

Soften Cracked or Dry Heels

Reduce Stretch Marks During Pregnancy

Shine Wooden Furniture

Untangle a Necklace Chain

Remove Bubblegum, Wax, or Band-aids

Have you heard that joke about baby oil? The one that goes something like:

If corn oil is made with corn and peanut oil is made with peanuts, then what is baby oil made with?

The answer: Baby oil is made with mineral oil and fragrance by industrial professionals; babies don't have the fine motor skills or chemistry knowledge to create baby oil, duh.

Baby oil is useful for a lot of things beyond baby bottoms. It'll smooth, soften, lubricate, refinish, clean, and so much more. It also has some usual uses for which it really oughtn't be used. Read on for some tips and tricks that'll help you step your baby oil game up.

But First, Some Don'ts

Don't use baby oil as a "personal" lubricant, particularly if you are using a latex condom. (Just look at the next step to see who wins in the latex vs. baby oil battle royale.)

Don't use baby oil to tan. Melanoma looks bad enough without being shiny.

Don't eat baby oil. It has laxative properties and likely doesn't taste delicious. (Mineral oil is safe for human consumption, but only up to around 100 mg. Many of those milligrams come from food-grade mineral oil that's used in baking and other industrial food-processing places because it's odorless and tasteless. My guess is that baby oil isn't food-grade. Stay safe—don't guzzle a bottle of it.)

Don't use it in your two-stroke engine.

Use 1: Get Latex Paint Off of Skin

I've worked as a painter for a couple of years, and every day was the same: I ended up with paint on me. Somewhere.

Latex paints and primers are sneaky. Sometimes they just rub off like rubber cement, other times they'll stay in your knuckles for a couple of days. Whenever some Lava soap couldn't get all the Lemon Ice or Chesapeake Gray paint off of my hands, baby oil would come to the rescue.

Rub a little onto the part of your body covered in paint using a cotton ball, shop towel, napkin, or anything else you've got on hand that will absorb the baby oil. Rub in concentric circles from the outside in without applying too much pressure. This isn't a scrub; it's more a gentle, localized massage. You can scrub to your heart's content after you've washed it off with some soap and water, once you feel you've made some progress with the oil.

This worked when I dropped a five gallon bucket of paint on myself while on a ladder. Because five gallons manages to get past the normal problem areas (hands, arms, flecks on the face from rolling out a ceiling) and into some unusual locations that could be sensitive to paint thinner, baby oil came in handy that day. Presumably the oil degrades the latex to the point that it will flake off. This is why condom + baby oil = one beautiful bundle of joy nine months later.

Use 2: Massage Oil

Use it as a massage oil. Remember our latex lessons from the previous step. Rubber gloves will degrade, as will balloons and some parts of massager attachments.

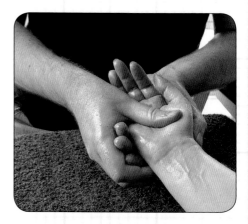

Use 3: Remove Earwax

When in-ear headphones were just starting to become a thing, I went deaf in one ear. Panicked, I went to the doctor only to discover that I had a cerumen compaction, i.e., earwax clogging my ear to the point that I couldn't hear. Gross, right?

For the temporarily hearing impaired, there's an easy home remedy to handle that waxy buildup: baby oil!

While lying on your side or tilting your head so your affected ear is up, drop five drops of baby oil (warmed, if you really want to dissolve the mess) inside your ear. Let it stay for long enough to dissolve some of the wax, then let the oil drain out onto a clean towel or into the sink. A small amount of warm water can be used to dislodge any last bits with a small bulb or needle-less syringe.

Use 4: Take Off Eye Makeup

Put some baby oil on a cotton ball. Gently rub it over any eye makeup that you want to remove. Maybe use another cotton ball to wipe away any excess oil.

This one does double duty: It removes makeup and makes your eyelids soft and supple.

Use 5: Bath Oil

Put a few drops into the next bath you draw. It'll leave your skin feeling soft and silky, though it may not prevent pruning in the extremities.

Use 6: Post-Shave Oil

Use as an after-shave oil after shaving any non-face part of the body. Works best as a layer over the top of some traditional moisturizer to lock in the freshness.

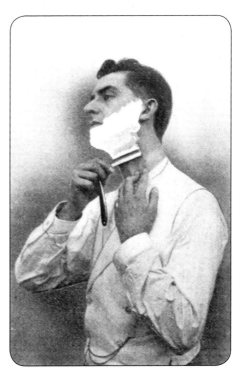

Use 7: Keep Warm

My little sister went to school in Montana. The temperature routinely dropped below −10 degrees Celsius. She would use baby oil or Vaseline as an extra layer of insulation on any exposed skin as she hiked her way to class. It apparently prevented any facial frostbite, as she still has her nose attached.

There are limits to how helpful or practical this is. You can't just grease up and head out in your skivvies when birds are dropping from trees encased in ice. But your mileage may vary.

Use 8: Soften Cracked or Dry Heels

If your heels are cracked, dry, and unsightly, baby oil and a sock will help. (I recognize that these two items are often used in conjunction for other purposes: filming extra-slippery versions of the Risky Business slide, freshening up a pair of stinky socks, and even—though I hesitate to mention it—cleaning off the sides of a dribble-y bottle of baby oil.)

Apply some baby oil over your heel before bed, put on some socks, then wake up transformed like a Jergens-Kafka mash-up.

Use 9: Reduce Stretch Marks During Pregnancy

Apply some baby oil to soften skin and prevent stretch marks during pregnancy. I hear good things about cocoa butter as well. Shea butter. Anything greasy and easily-absorbent.

But baby oil is perfect, since you're applying the oil directly to the baby's temporary home.

Use 10: Shine Wooden Furniture

If your dinner party is starting in 10 minutes and you've just noticed that there are hideous water stains on your tabletops, have no fear. Baby oil can help by providing a quick polish.

The mineral oil will put a nice shine on the furniture, helping to create a waterproof barrier and an understated shine that should impress any and all guests. Plus, it'll smell fresh and baby-like.

Use 11: Untangle a Necklace Chain

You find a snarl in your necklace that seems impossible to undo. Before you throw away your diamonds and gold in frustration, try a quick baby oil bath. It'll lubricate the metal links, allowing them to separate more easily. Use a pin to work out the tangled knot after the dunk in oil.

Presto! You just saved a couple grand by not throwing away your jewelry. You're welcome.

Use 12: Remove Bubblegum, Wax, or Band-aids

If you've got some bubblegum or wax on your body or in your hair, baby oil will get it out. Apply a small amount to the affected area, let it sit, then work at the mess with your fingertips. It'll make gum easier to get out, it'll soften wax, and it will help a bandage come off without tearing out any hair.

This is a particularly good method of removing excess wax after an eyebrow or bikini job.

For those of you who remove more band-aids than body hair, applying some baby oil around the bandage is a great middle-of-the-road option for people who can't subscribe to the RIP IT OFF! camp or the IT'LL FALL OFF ON ITS OWN, DON'T TOUCH IT! contingent. Firm but gentle, that's the way to do it. Tough love.

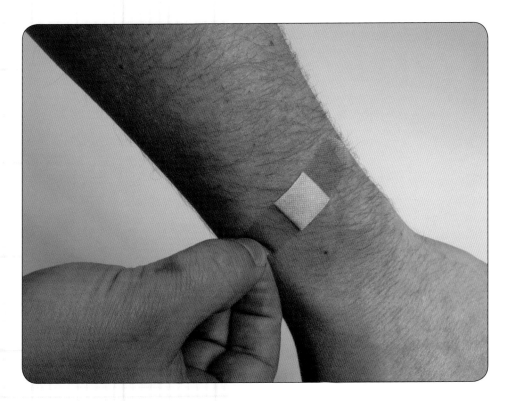

9 Unusual Uses for Toothpaste

By Wade Wilgus (wilgubeast)

(http://www.instructables.com/id/9-Unusual-Uses-for-Toothpaste/)

Spackle Those Drywall Holes

Phineas DeFogger

Unscuff Your Air Force Ones, Murphy Lee

Clean Your Iron

Polish Jewelry

Shine up Your Hog

Clean the Sink

Save CDs

Spot Treatment

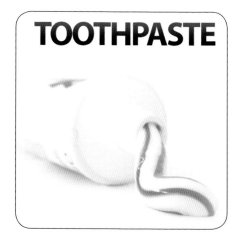

Toothpaste. It keeps your teeth from rotting and falling out of your face. It makes you eligible for kisses you otherwise wouldn't qualify for. And it ensures that you drink your morning orange juice *before* brushing.

But it's got other uses. It can save you money, make you seem like a better roommate than you are, or rescue your TLC and Alanis Morissette CDs. Read on for some unusual uses of toothpaste.

Use 1: Spackle Those Drywall Holes

It was 10:45 and my landlord was supposed to come around at 11:00 to do a final walkthrough of the apartment to determine if I would get back my sizeable security deposit. My place was so clean that the radiator and vertical slat blinds seemed oddly prominent, but there was still something off. I hadn't partied with Mötley Crüe, I wasn't hoarding cats, and the burglars left surprisingly little damage once the broken window was cleaned up.

10:46. I'm wishing I had studied *Highlights for Children* more diligently while I waited to see my dentist. What's wrong with this picture?

Oh . . . there are a series of holes in the walls ranging in size from very tiny to small. Stupid picture frames, calendar nail, and curtain rods. Why didn't I realize that I would have to move out eventually and fill all of these holes? It's already 10:48?!

What to do what to do what to do . . . spackle. I need something spackle-y. Something white and pasty and . . . that's it! Toothpaste to the rescue. A quick dab here, a gentle smoosh there, and voilá! Handled.

11:15. Full deposit returned in exchange for my minty-fresh apartment. Cashier's check, you and I are going to the bank before the toothpaste dries.

Use 2: Phineas DeFogger

I am a terrible swimmer. I am scared of the water and predatory sea creatures freak me out. So, naturally, I went scuba diving, uncertified, when I was 17. Besides abject terror, the biggest problem I had was with my mask fogging up like a strip mall Bikram yoga studio. At least I couldn't see the vicious clown fish and sea anemones trying to eat me whole.

Luckily, toothpaste can be used on a new glass mask[3] to remove any residue left over from the lens mounting or manufacturing process that would allow a buildup of blinding fog to ruin an otherwise delightful and terrifying dive. The fine abrasive in regular old white, non-gel toothpaste can be used to scrub off the residue. Just wet the inside of the mask, then scrub (with an old toothbrush, perhaps?) it out thoroughly. Rinse completely with warm water.

To test your recently-defogged mask, run the lens under cold water until it's nice and chilly. Take the mask into your hands like a third date, then breathe heavily and moistly into it. There shouldn't be any foggy spots. If some popped up, repeat with the toothpaste until the mask is clean.

To keep the mask from fogging up in the future, use defogging solution, spit, or baby shampoo inside the mask. Now you'll see the menacing sponges before they manage to sneak up on you while you fumble with your regulator.

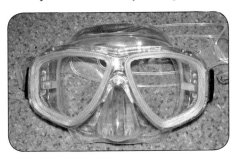

---

[3]Or pair of goggles. This tip works on regular old swimming goggles as well. But the ocean is far sexier than the black line at the bottom of a pool, so I focused on scuba masks. Sorry Michael Phelps.

Use 3: Unscuff Your Air Force Ones, Murphy Lee

A fresh pair of clean kicks just make your day, don't they? They'll put some dip in your hips, some cut in your strut, and some glide in your stride. But the honeymoon fades fast when your fine pair of sneakers get scuff marks all around the foxing.[4] Your once proud gait is reduced to a miserable shuffle, all because you scuffed your shoe on a raised bit of curb.

Fear not, friends, because a little bit of toothpaste will right all wrongs. Just brush the side of your shoe with a touch of toothpaste to take out those pernicious blemishes. With some elbow grease and some toothpaste, you'll be back to strolling and sauntering with sass.

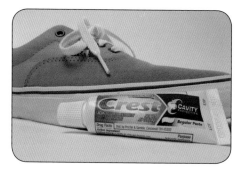

Use 4: Clean Your Iron

I hate ironing. I am vigilant in the laundry room, trying to pull out my button-downs while they're still warm in order to immediately get them onto a hanger. I'd rather hang things like crazy than have to pull out the board and the iron and the spray bottle. But sometimes I mess up the timing and my shirts and pants are Willy Loman rumpled. Even the iron-free ones.

Because my ironing skills are poor to mediocre, my iron sometimes gets gunky. Normally, I would let it collect grime and forget about it, but I had some extra toothpaste and a whimsical thought: Maybe some toothpaste will clean this off. Sure enough, a little scrub with toothpaste and the iron is as good as new (which is great for those times when I'm 30 seconds late to collect my clothes from the dryer on a Sunday night, and one of my neighbors has placed my permanent press items unceremoniously into a pile on the folding counter).

Use 5: Polish Jewelry

The iron isn't the only thing that toothpaste will polish. Are your diamond rings so filthy they look like zirconia? Scrub 'em with some toothpaste and rinse. You'll be burning retinas in no time. Is your watch trying to tell you the time, but the bezel and band are so nasty that it looks like you're wearing a chunky bracelet, possibly made of felt or aged leather? Rub it down with a dry

---

[4] This trick works for white leather as well, not just the rubber foxing on your plimsolls.

cloth and some toothpaste to knock off the dirt. Your Fossil won't be mistaken for a Rolex, but at least you'll know how late you're running.

Use 6: Shine up Your Hog

Continuing our shining kick, toothpaste will shine chrome, too. When riding your hog through the mean streets of the San Francisco financial district, you'll sometimes get a little somethin'-somethin' on your pipes. Use a paper towel or soft cloth to rub on some toothpaste, then wipe it off. Your pipes will gleam, and you might even be more visible to the oblivious cars wanting to change lines through you and your bike.

Use 7: Clean the Sink

This is a use that everyone has probably come across at some point in their tooth-brushing lives.

When you drop a glob of toothpaste into the sink, you can rub it around to clean the area around the drain, the faucet, and the basin. The mess becomes the cleaning agent. This is awesome.

I have been routinely complimented for how clean I keep my bathrooms, and this is the only reason. Toothpaste is literally at hand. No digging through cleaning products, no searching for a sponge, just my fingers and the toothpaste that I accidentally let fall off of my brush/dribble out of my mouth onto the faucet.

Use 8: Save CDs

Some of you kids may not realize it, but once upon a time there were these things called "CDs" and "DVDs." They would occasionally get scratched and cause the music or movies on them to skip. With a tube of toothpaste and some luck, it is possible to rescue a scratched disc.

Put a small dab of toothpaste onto the scratched side of the disc. With a soft, clean towel, rub the toothpaste over the entire disc in concentric circles, as though you were the needle on a record player.[5] Wipe any remaining toothpaste off with a slightly-damp towel. You could be listening to "Tubthumping" on repeat in no time.

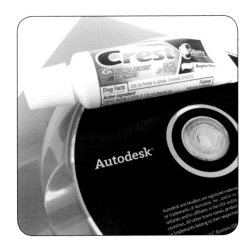

---

[5] Ask your grandparents what a "record" is.

Use 9: Spot Treatment

Oh no! The big dance/meeting/presentation/date is tomorrow, and you have a zit blossoming like a third eye in the center of your forehead. Instead of ignoring it or popping it and hoping for the best, try this little trick with some toothpaste.

Put a dab of it onto the blemish before bedtime. The pimple should shrink in size and diminish in redness by morning, so you can go about your day without resorting to bangs like that girl from *The Ring* or Justin Bieber.

(This is assuming that you aren't a chronic sufferer of acne who already has an arsenal of chemical weapons to destroy any whiteheads, blackheads, zits, pimples, spots, or blemishes that might dare to erupt on your face. Or that you don't have any aspirin.)

6 Ways Medicated Chest Rub Will Save Your Relationship

By Karen Howard
(http://www.instructables.com/id/
How-Medicated-Chest-Rub-Will-Help-Save-Your-Relati/)

A Classic Decongestant

Play Footsie Again

Not Tonight Honey, I Have a Headache . . .

It's Not You, It's Your Cat

"You Don't Know Why I'm Crying?!"

Lipstick on His Collar?

Remember: Proceed with Caution

Let's face it: There has been some tension lately. Every relationship goes through its ups and downs, but let's take the passive route this time, and avoid one of those "we need to talk" confrontations. Ugh.

Luckily, with just a small amount of medicated vaporizing chest rub, your relationship woes can be squashed before any serious conversation needs to happen. Who knew? Thanks, Vicks!

Use 1: A Classic Decongestant

I'll just get the obvious use out of the way: VapoRub can do wonders for your beauty rest. If your partner is snoring or hacking up a storm all night, just rub a little Vicks on their chest so they'll shut up. You'll be back to counting sheep in no time.

Otherwise, I hear the couch is a relatively comfortable sleeping option. For them, of course.

Use 2: Play Footsie Again

Does it feel like the magic's gone? Has that spark fizzled?

Back when you were first dating, you couldn't keep your hands, or toes for that matter, off of each other. But now your partner's funky feet couldn't be more of a turn off. Nasty.

While VapoRub was originally intended for your sinuses, it has a surprising amount of uses further south on those sore puppies. If you or your partner have lately kept the socks on while things have been getting hot-and-heavy, it might be time to take further action and stop being embarrassed.

Heels dry and cracked? Tell your loved one to keep these rough soles away from you and to rub Vicks on them instead. They should heal up after a few treatments—and smell menthol fresh!

While having an athletic partner can certainly have its pluses, athlete's foot is a major no-no. VapoRub clears this up in no time.

Toenail fungus getting you down? Massage chest rub on the affected toenails once or twice daily. They'll eventually turn dark, but don't worry! This just means you're killing the fungus. As you continue to trim your toenails, you'll soon find them growing in free of fungus and in great shape.

Now that you both can wear sandals again, maybe it's time to bring that tropical vacation idea back to the table.

Use 3: Not Tonight Honey, I Have a Headache . . .

. . . no, but really.

If you're not making excuses and are actually feeling some pain, rub a little Vick's on your temples, or under your nose if it's a sinus headache. Drink some water, take an aspirin or two, and you should be able to get back to those more enjoyable things in no time.

Use 4: It's Not You, It's Your Cat

Some people are dog people. Some people are cat people. These differences are what make life so exciting.

But when you asked your partner to move in and to bring Mr. Whiskers along, you weren't expecting him to be such a furry feline menace. He's scratching up your couch, peeing all over your carpet, and seems to think of your legs as his personal climbing tree. I know you're angry, but there's no need to take drastic measures.

Cats detest the menthol and eucalyptus smells in Vicks, and, as you're starting to detest Miss Kitty and everything she stands for, it seems only fitting to smear chest rub all over those things she loves. She'll steer clear from now on. Just a small amount does wonders, and it won't do any more damage to your drapes than that tiny bobcat already has.

Use 5: "You Don't Know Why I'm Crying?!"

Sometimes a little drama can go a long way. If you need some added leverage in your relationship, and think feigning tears would do the trick, take a page out of Acting 101's book and grab that chest rub. Dab just a tiny bit below your eyes, and, as the vapors rise up, you'll start tearing. Now whip out those fake sobs and get to negotiating.

Use 6: Lipstick on His Collar?

If you suspect your man of cheating, perhaps it's time to take matters into your own hands.

Many professional race horse owners swear by chest rub as a way to keep their male horses focused on their training. When spring is in the air, and all the fine young lady horses are emitting powerful estrus pheromones, many trainers will rub Vicks on the males' noses. The strong medicated smell completely overpowers those natural feminine perfumes, and the boys can get back to business.

If he's been acting suspicious lately, but you don't feel like asking the hard question, rub some VapoRub under his nose and he'll be your personal stallion once more.

Remember: Proceed with Caution

Take some care when working with chest rub, because you don't want to get Vicks in your eye (or any orifice/sensitive place for that matter. Yes, I'm talking to you folks who really want to get creative with this mentholated rub. I know what you're thinking . . . and it's a horrible idea). Chest rub can cause some serious damage if used improperly. VapoRub contains camphor, among other things, which is poisonous if ingested. There are people out there who swear by Vicks as a cure for acne, paper cuts, splinters, chapped lips, or even hemorrhoids. As always, please consult your doctor before self-medicating.

Section 4

From the Vanity

10 Unusual Uses for Moustaches

By Mike Warren (mikeasaurus)

(http://www.instructables.com/id/unusual-uses-for-moustaches/)

Disguise

Soup Strainer

Decision Maker

Cookie Duster

Mustache Rides

New Trichotillomania Site

Shoe/Nail/Dish Brush

Foamy Frappe Remover

Air Bubble Retention

Chin Puppet

Bonus! A Fresh Face

Moustaches are wonderful things. They can be groomed, grown wild, or printed to novelty-size and applied in suspicious places. Many famous men (and some women) from history have owed their notoriety to their unmistakable moustaches. I wanted to join the ranks of these prestigious moustaches and decided to grow my own and explore the things I could achieve with my new face fur.

After growing a full beard I shaved it into a rakish moustache, sure to tantalize even the most fickle mustachio aficionado. I soon noticed a change all around me—everywhere I went, women were mesmerized and drawn to me, and men wanted to duel in the streets. Whoa, moustaches have a strange, powerful effect on people.

Don't take my word for it? Here's some interesting trivia about just how awesome moustaches are:

- In a standard deck of playing cards the King of Hearts is the only king without a moustache.
- Scientific research, commissioned by the Guinness Brewing Company, found that the average mustachioed Guinness drinker traps a pint and a half of beer in his moustache every year.
- On average a man with a moustache touches it 760 times in a twenty-four-hour time period.
- The oldest artifact portraying a moustache was from 300 BC.
- Burt Reynolds is widely considered the world's "Manliest Man" (c.1972), due in no small part to his full moustache.
- Men with moustaches are better lovers. Okay, I made that one up.

Trivia aside, moustaches have defined great men and their identities for centuries: Nietzsche, Dali, Einstein, Hulk Hogan . . . and now, me! But, aside from looking devilishly handsome and irresistible, what else can you do with your moustache?

Follow along and learn ten unusual uses for moustaches!

Use 1: Disguise

Probably the single greatest attribute your moustache can lend you is the ability to disguise yourself: a novelty hat, a few odd garments, and you have yourself an instant disguise.

Classic disguise

Here we have a classic example of someone who would seamlessly blend into any background. Non-descriptive bland clothing, oversize hat, mirrored-shades, and a moustache—who was that man? Maybe we'll never know.

Villain

Nothing makes you look more sinister than a devious moustache. I could probably trust this guy if it wasn't for the moustache. I mean look at him: Cape, top hat, cane, he could be a magician . . . wait a minute. Is that a moustache? He went from possible magic performer to the antagonist from just about every episode of *Rocky and Bullwinkle*.

'80s cred

If wearing white shutter-shades, high-boxed baseball caps, and neon isn't enough, throw a moustache into the mix and *bam!*—automatic 80s credentials. You'll look so authentic, Marty McFly wouldn't even question which time you're from. Make sure you make that awkward 80s face we all made back then, too—it really sells the look.

Use 2: Soup Strainer

Don't you hate it when your thick soup separates while it's cooling and all the floaty bits rise to the top? That first sip is always so unpleasant, if only there was some way to strain out those pesky floaty bits and get to the tender goodies hidden under the top layer. Enter, moustache!

If you let your lip-fur grow untamed, eventually the hairs will grow past your upper lip and form a sieve before your mouth, kind of like how blue whales strain out krill. Your floaty bits would be the soup equivalent to krill, and you, dear reader, would be the whale.

Use 3: Decision Maker

If I've learned anything from *Dateline* and Fox News, it's that moustached, faceless, multinational companies are running the world and making all the decisions on my behalf. Obviously, I was powerless to stop this before, but my new moustache gave me the perfect "in." Wearing some important-looking clothing, I managed to sneak my way into a few upper-echelon meetings.

During my time in some high-glossed cedar-walled office, I waxed on about "how Q2 was under-performing due to new tax legislation" and that "the new CAO had not yet received adequate consultation on the last GIPS." The other corporate Bigwigs and I hobnobbed for a while; we laughed some, drank a snifter of brandy, and smoked a cigar. I made sure to fire a few people, too, before I left, for good measure.

Making important decisions is hard, but moustache and I pulled it off like pros.

Use 4: Cookie Duster

After all those important decisions it was time for a cookie or two (finally).

The only ones I could find were some old, dusty ones hidden in the back of the cupboard. Sensing that my moustache was becoming hungry, I decided that eating them would be wiser then not eating them—thereby upsetting my new mouth-friend—despite the amount of dirt that had accumulated on top of each cookie.

My moustache was only too happy to help out, carefully dusting the top of each one before entering my mouth. While my moustache swept, I enjoyed clean (albeit stale) cookies. What a team!

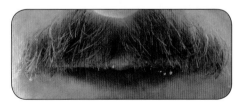

Use 5: Mustache Rides

After growing my moustache, I noticed that I started to have some really strange dreams. There's this one reoccurring dream I have where I'm Aladdin flying on my trusty carpet. Except this was a really weird carpet made out of animal fur and shaped like a boomerang, and we just kept going back and forth to this cave in the desert to collect scarabs.

I don't know what that means, and even the roadside-gypsy I later consulted about an interpretation was dumbstruck.

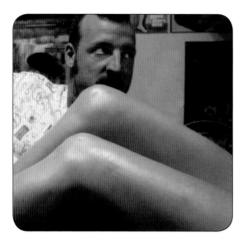

Use 6: New Trichotillomania Site

Maybe you're not content with pulling your scalp or sideburns. Everyone with trichotillomania would probably love to have a new site to discover. To be honest, I suffer from this. It's totally subconscious and more facial hair made it worse; a full beard almost destroyed my face.

Seriously, Mike, stop it.

Use 7: Shoe/Nail/Dish Brush

The hair on my head is just like my moustache—various colors and thick. I've been told my head hair reminds people of a beaver's pelt or a Brillo Pad. With this in mind, I set to task looking for ways my handsome hirsute 'stache could be put to use.

Shoe polish application

I discovered that my moustache was perfect for applying a good coat of polish to my nice dress shoes. The grain of the leather really took the polish with the application from such a stiff, natural bush.

Nail brush

My nails were covered with compound after applying the polish, so I took a shower and managed to get my nails clean while cleaning my moustache!

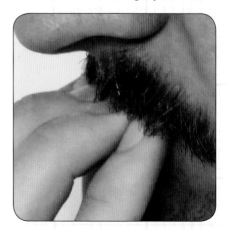

Dishes

Later that evening it was my turn to help wash the dishes. Regrettably, my moustache volunteered before I could and I ended up washing dishes with my moustache until my face became all pruney.

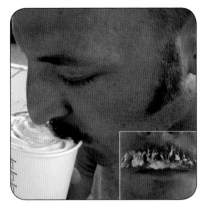

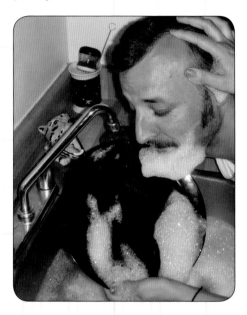

Use 8: Foamy Frappe Remover

Ever notice that when you order your ventisoy milk extras hot no fat caramel frappuccino, it always seems like you have to mine your way through all that foam to get to your goods? I mean, I'd ask them not to give me so much whip if the barista could hear me over everyone shouting orders all over the place. Instead, I just endure and wait in the crowded Starbizzle for my oversized, foamy mess and ponder how to consume.

Only, today it's different. I came prepared with my own foamy frappe remover! My moustache was able to hold back the tasty topping and allow me to get to the frozen, caffeinated goodness below.

Teamwork is a beautiful thing.

Use 9: Air Bubble Retention

How many times have I found myself in a near-death drowning situation, wishing I had a few extra bubbles nearby for that last little bit of air? Seriously, it's like a weekly occurrence.

Depending on how long your moustache is, it may be long enough to trap air bubbles, thereby giving you a few additional precious seconds to stay underwater and evade capture. It's just like in A View to a Kill with James Bond, except you're not using a car tire to stay alive, just the air your moustache has trapped on your descent. Which is probably plenty, or at least more than your smooth-faced comrades.

Just look at the pictures; I can see at least three solid bubbles there. That's got to be . . . what, 5 minutes of air? With all these bubbles around and my moustache-cum-air-trapper, you might as well just give me a snorkel.

Use 10: Chin Puppet

With a little change in orientation and some artistically-applied makeup, your moustache can also double as the beard for a chin puppet. Draw a small face upside down on your chin, then add a few embellishments, and your upside down face can be transformed into a chin puppet. My moustache lent itself perfectly as a chin-beard for a gnome character—we even made him a little gnome hat!

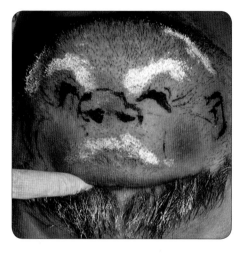

Bonus! A Fresh Face

Now that you've had a fun time scaring children and showing up on police blotters, it's time to retire the tuft. Be thankful for the time you spent together and the new experiences that came because of it: You dusted cookies, you made shoes shine, you were a majestic blue whale, a global executive with a VSOP collection. You were a god among men. In reality, it was mostly scared screams, double-takes, and crying infants.

Through my moustache travels, I discovered that, though some women find the allure and mystique of a moustached man irresistible, most prefer a smooth shave to nuzzle up to. After shaving my face, I went looking for a big sloppy kiss to try and authenticate my smooth-face theory. Being single, I had to improvise for this picture, but you get the idea.

8 Incredible Eye Makeup Remover Hacks

By Carley Jacobson (Carleyy)
(http://www.instructables.com/id/
8-Incredible-Eye-Makeup-Remover-Hacks/)

Here are eight easy ways to make homemade hacks for removing your eye makeup! You can find all of these ingredients lying around your house and in your local health food store.

I have tried each of these on myself and they all work just as good as any eye makeup remover I have bought at the drug store. Try them out for yourself!

Use 1: Avocados

I found a lot of recipes for eye makeup remover that called for avocado oil. I had some avocados lying around the kitchen . . . thus, avocado oil!

For this, I just took a Q-tip and swabbed the avocado. You don't need to get a chunk of avocado on the Q-tip; just coat it in the oil from the avocado.

Use 2: No-Tears Baby Shampoo

Just add a drop of baby shampoo to a cotton pad or swab to remove eye makeup. I bought this little bottle for less than $2. What a great deal if you consider how much money you pay for eye makeup remover!

Use 3: Hair Conditioner

You already have it in your bathroom. Just a little dab of hair conditioner does the job!

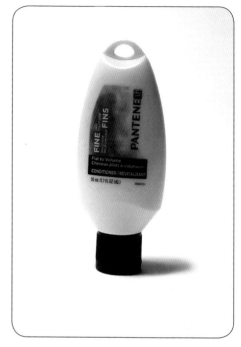

Use 4: Shortening

Shortening? It's just vegetable oil, and it keeps your skin soft. When your makeup remover runs out, just run to your kitchen for some makeshift eye makeup remover.

Use 5: Petroleum Jelly

A little bit goes a long way! Petroleum jelly is a safe way to remove your waterproof makeup. Use just a small amount to remove your eye makeup, then go ahead and dab some on your lips!

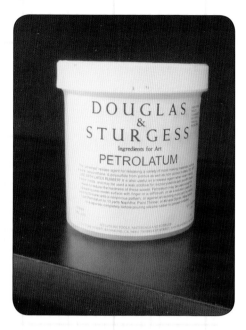

Use 6: Grape Seed and Castor Oil

Recipe
- 3 tbsp. grape seed oil
- 1 tbsp. castor oil

Mix these oils together in a cup and stir. This is a great recipe for sensitive skin.

Use 7: Jojoba Oil

Recipe
- 1 part jojoba oil
- 2 parts water

Try this sustainably friendly makeup remover! It is non-allergenic, so it is perfect for use on eyes. It can also be used to remove any other makeup.

Use 8: Vegetable Oil Medley

Recipe

Combine equal parts olive oil, canola oil, and castor oil (I used a tbsp of each).

These vegetable oils blend together to create the perfect eye makeup remover!

Final Test—Which Produces the Best Results?

I tested all of these on my eyes, but I wanted to see how they compared.

I put eight eyeliner marks on my arm (first picture). Then I dipped a cotton swab in each mixture and lightly rubbed it on the eyeliner ten times. You can still see the eyeliner for each remover in the second picture because I did not wipe away the residue after I applied it (which you would normally do with any eye makeup remover).

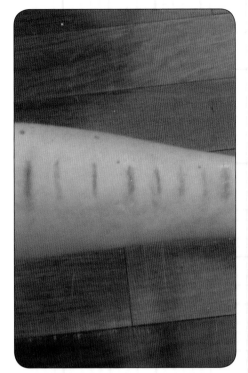

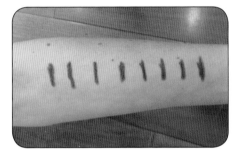

10 Unusual Uses for Nail Polish

By Carley Jacobson (Carleyy)

(http://www.instructables.com/id/10-Unusual-Uses-for-Nail-Polish/)

Smudge-Proof Labels

Seal an Envelope

Threading a Needle

Prevent Costume Jewelry from Tarnishing

Keep Laces and Rope from Unraveling

Tighten Loose Screws

Color-Code Objects

Mark Levels in a Bucket

Rustproof Metal

Liquid Band-Aid

If you're anything like me, you have bottles of nail polish building up in your desk drawer from years ago. What you might not know is that there are plenty of ways to put that nail polish to use besides just decorating your fingers. Here are ten new uses for nail polish that will help you with day-to-day tasks around the house!

Use 1: Smudge-Proof Labels

Prevent ink from running on your labels. Coat the labels that identify your garden plants or the labels that distinguish your shampoo bottles with clear nail polish.

Use 2: Seal an Envelope

Ever see that episode of *Seinfeld* where George's fiancée dies from licking too many wedding invitations?

Avoid licking that gross glue on the back of an envelope. Just seal it with a little bit of clear nail polish.

Use 3: Threading a Needle

It can be a pain in the butt trying to thread a needle! I know I have had my moments where I've had to walk away from projects because it gets too frustrating. A quick fix for this is dipping the end of your thread in a small amount of nail polish for easy thread-ability.

Use 4: Prevent Costume Jewelry from Tarnishing

Ever get those green rings on your fingers from wearing a costume ring? Paint a thin coat of clear nail polish on your costume jewelry to prevent tarnishing.

Use 5: Keep Laces and Rope from Unraveling

You may have heard that burning the ends of cut rope prevent it from fraying. Nail polish works just as well! Just coat the ends of your shoe laces or rope with clear nail polish (or colored nail polish for some fun) to prevent any fraying.

Use 6: Tighten Loose Screws

For an extra hold, coat your screws in nail polish. After setting the screws, let the polish dry. This should give you added durability.

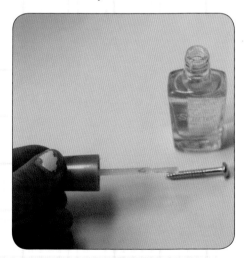

Use 7: Color-Code Objects

Color code objects to easily distinguish them. I color coded my keys with nail polish so I can quickly figure out which key is for my front door!

Use 8: Mark Levels in a Bucket

Mark levels on measuring cups or buckets. For your cleaning bucket, you can mark a level for how much soap you need and another level for how much water you need.

Use 9: Rustproof Metal

Apply clear nail polish to metals that are vulnerable to rusting, i.e., in the bathroom or outdoors.

Some ideas:
- Shaving cream: If your shaving cream can creates rust rings on your bath tub, apply a thin layer of nail polish to the bottom.
- Screws in patio furniture or the toilet
- Car Paint: Keep chipped car paint from rusting by coating the damaged areas with nail polish.

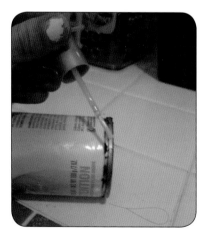

Use 10: Liquid Band-Aid

I heard this one from **Scoochmaroo**! She uses clear nail polish as a liquid band-aid. Apparently it's the same thing . . . who knew!

6 Underappreciated Things About Petroleum Jelly

By Gregg Horton (frenzy)

(http://www.instructables.com/id/6-under-appreciated-things-about-Petroleum-Jelly/)

- Prevent Light Bulbs from Sticking

- Open Your Shower Quicker

- Loosen Stuck Drawers

- Remove Squeak from Door Hinges

- Starting a Fire

- Replacement Chapstick

Every house has a jar of good ol' petroleum jelly. Yet this jelly is very underappreciated for all of its great uses. Here are a few of the most interesting!

Use 1: Prevent Light Bulbs from Sticking

A common problem with outdoor light bulbs is that they tend to stick to the fixture. If this happens, trying to get out the bulb might end up in it breaking. Put some petroleum jelly around the threads before putting the bulb in to allow for easy removal later.

Use 2: Open Your Shower Quicker

Having a hard time rushing out of the shower? Put some petroleum jelly on your curtain rod in your shower to open your curtain lightning fast!

Use 3: Loosen Stuck Drawers

Have a stuck drawer? Use petroleum jelly to prevent it from sticking and make the drawer move smoother.

Use 4: Remove Squeak from Door Hinges

A bit of petroleum jelly on a door hinge can take away that annoying squeak. Then you can sneak around your home effectively.

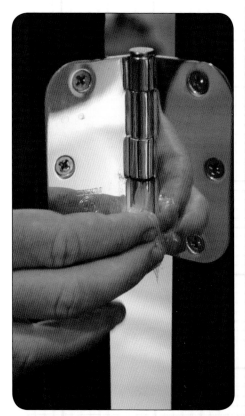

Use 5: Starting a Fire

You can use petroleum jelly to help you start a fire. It works pretty well with stuff that is having a hard time starting.

Use 6: Replacement Chapstick

If you run out of chapstick, petroleum jelly is a great lip moisturizer. Just apply liberally to the lips and *BAM!* no more chapped lips!

13 Unusual Uses for a Hair Dryer

By Carley Jacobson (Carleyy)
(http://www.instructables.com/id/13-Unusual-Uses-for-a-Hair-Dryer/)

Remove Stickers and Price Tags

Custom Fit Your Glasses

Wax on *Wax Off*

Add Gloss to Cake Frosting

Dry Clothing

Dry Steam Off of Mirror

Remove Dust

Hot Compress

Remove Crayon Marks from Walls

Dry Wet Boots

Thaw Window Frames

Dry Painted Nails

Defrosting Food

A HAIR DRYER

Oh, the unusual things you can do with your house hold gadgets! I've thoroughly researched all the strange and weird uses for your hair dryer. Yes, that's correct: hair dryer. Fitting your glasses to your head and adding a glaze to your cake frosting are just some of the unusual uses I discovered.

You can tell from the look on my face that this is no joke.

Use 1: Remove Stickers and Price Tags

Have you ever spent hours peeling a sticker off of a window or box? You scratch it but only small bits of paper come off. . . .

The hot air from a hair dryer will loosen a price tag or sticker, making removal super easy. You can also use this trick to remove contact paper from shelves.

Use 2: Custom Fit Your Glasses

Custom fit your plastic frame glasses. Simply heat up the ends and mold them to fit our head.

This works great on store-bought glasses. I wouldn't recommend this for your $300 designer frames.

Use 3: Wax on *Wax Off*

Getting candle wax on wood furniture can be a nightmare to get off. (Again with the scratching!) The best way to remove it is to heat it back up. Blow medium heat on the wax until it starts to melt, then wipe it away with a cloth.

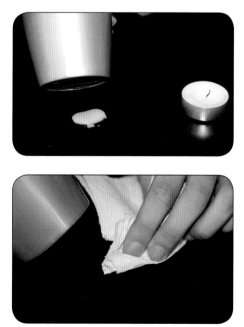

Use 4: Add Gloss to Cake Frosting

Give your baked good a professional-looking gloss. Turn your dryer on low heat and slowly blow it over the entire cake.

Use 5: Dry Clothing

Quickly dry spots of water you spilt on your clothes. First, *remove the article of clothing*—you don't want any burns on your skin! Hang it over a shower rod and dry.

If this happens at a party, I fully encourage snooping through your friend's bathroom cabinets for a dryer.

Use 6: Dry Steam Off of Mirror

It's frustrating to lose mirror access after a steamy shower! Dry that steam off with a quick blast of hot air from your hair dryer. Now you can just leave the blow dryer on and continue drying your hair.

Use 7: Remove Dust

Use a hair dryer to remove dust from hard to get to nooks and crannies in your house. Use this trick on carved woodwork, art work, artificial flowers, bookshelves, lamps, computers . . . you name it!

Use 8: Hot Compress

Keep a hot compress hot by pointing your blow dryer at the towel and leaving it running while you are putting the compress on an injury. Keep the towel wet by misting it with a spray bottle.

Use 10: Dry Wet Boots

This is a great trick to use in the winter! Dry off your snowy boots with your blow dryer setting on high. Be sure to do this over a towel so your mom doesn't yell at you for getting water everywhere! (Personal experience . . .)

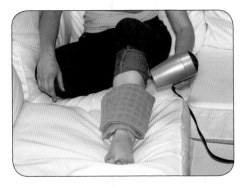

Use 9: Remove Crayon Marks from Walls

If you read step three, then you can understand why this makes sense.

Crayons are made out of wax, hair dryers remove wax, thus hair dryers remove crayons.

Set the hair dryer on hot and keep it on the crayon mark until it melts. The crayon will wipe off easily with a damp cloth and a small amount of oil soap cleanser.

Use 11: Thaw Window Frames

Here is another wintertime use. If you forgot to put your storm windows down in time for the first snow and your windows freeze shut before you can get to them, thaw your window frame with a blast from your hair dryer. Then open, tug down your storm window, and promptly close.

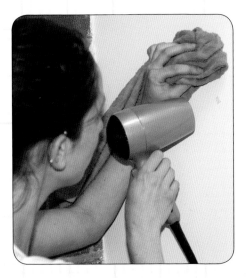

Use 12: Dry Painted Nails

I love painting my nails, but I have so much trouble waiting for my nails to air dry. A tip for quickly drying your painted nails: Blow dry them! Not too high of a setting, just a little hot air to speed the process up.

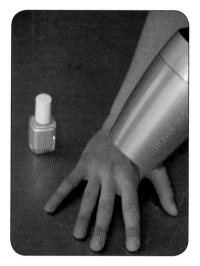

Use 13: Defrosting Food

I have had bags of peas freeze to the side of my freezer. It's super frustrating and I hate having to chip away at ice mounds with my hands. Make this process easier by melting the ice with a blow dryer.

Section 5

From the Closet

11 Unusual Uses for Tennis Balls

By Wade Wilgus (wilgubeast)
(http://www.instructables.com/id/10-Unusual-Uses-for-Tennis-Balls/)

Protect Your Floors

Laundry

Garage Penetration Indicator

Pool Cleaner

Remove Floor Scuff Marks

Massager

Childproof Corners

Sand Curves

Jar Opener

Photo Mount

Put Stuff Inside

TENNIS BALLS

Tennis balls are ubiquitous and inexpensive. They're great for tennis . . . for a little while. Then they lose that carefree, Tigger-like bounciness and become dog toys.[6] But what if you don't have a dog? What can you do with some tennis balls? Laundry? Yeah. Household cleaning? Yep. Parking? Got you covered. Sensual self-massage? You bet your felted fluorescent balls.

Don't you worry, baby birds. I have chewed on this wooly problem for a while now, and I am ready to regurgitate my knowledge into your cheeping little maws. So let's help you fledge the nest and unlock the McEnroe/MacGyver potential you have buried deep inside your life-hacking soul.

Go grab some balls from the bushes behind the local tennis courts. Intercept a lobbed ball at the local dog park. Begin training as a Wimbledon ball-boy. Do whatever you need to do to get a hold of these magical golden orbs.

---

[6]According to small, panicky corners of the Internet, tennis balls may be bad for your dog's health. That fuzzy yellow coating might be ruining Fido's teeth. They're choking hazards for large dogs. They could randomly explode.

Use 1: Protect Your Floors

Refinishing a floor is a messy, time-consuming, and expensive task. It sucks, and you probably don't want to do it. I've done it professionally, and it's not even fun when you're being paid for it.

Protect your precious floors by capping chair legs, walker feet,[7] and pirate pegs that might need to consistently slide or tap across your floor. Just cut an X into the top of a tennis ball and insert the offending leg into the warm embrace of the tennis ball. Done.

Use 2: Laundry

I like my towels to be fluffy and absorbent, but I hate the smell and texture of clothes that have been laundered with fabric softening dryer sheets. In an attempt to ditch the dryer sheets, I decided to just go without. My clothes were fine, but my towels just weren't fluffy enough.

To fluff those towels, I decided to toss in a tennis ball. Or three. Just to see what would happen. Would they have the same effect as those made-for-TV dryer balls? Would they destroy the dryer? Would my neighbors complain about the *thunk*-ing noises?

Turns out, tennis balls make a *great* replacement for dryer sheets with regard to fluffification. Static prevention and scent, not so much. But those aren't necessary for my towels. Or comforter. Or any of my other giant linens that require fluffiness.

Use 3: Garage Penetration Indicator

Sometimes it can be difficult to pull into one's garage without crashing into the back wall. Even with daily practice, pulling into the garage can be a nerve-wracking experience. Sure, it's not landing an F-16 on the deck of an aircraft carrier, but it can be a tricky maneuver. Particularly for guest drivers. Or teens. Or anyone else who is secondary on your insurance forms.

To keep those fragile boxes full of Christmas decorations and sixth grade soccer participation trophies safe, why not dangle a tennis ball from your garage ceiling to mark where you should stop?

---

[7]You've probably seen this trick at the local senior hang-out. Probably alongside a rousing game of shuffleboard or aqua-robics. Walker feet covered in tennis balls facilitate safe sliding and are easier to replace/cheaper than little rubber caps.

Here's a way to do it[8]: Hang a string from where you think it will hit the center of your windshield or the spot right in front of the driver. Park better than you ever have before. Using a stick, laser pointer, friend, or your eyeballs, determine where you should hang your tennis ball. Put a screw into your sweet spot, and then tie on the string. Attach the string to the tennis ball. Then just remember to stop when you hit the tennis ball as you drive into your garage.

Use 4: Pool Cleaner

Swimming pools get nasty. The more people who swim in them, the thicker and more disgusting the slick of human grease that floats to the top of the pool. Those kids who are retrieving various weights from the bottom of the pool? They're avoiding the BP[9] oil sheen at the surface.

Tennis balls can help absorb some of that people oil. The felted surface collects the nasty goop from the surface of the water. Toss in a few balls if your private pool is looking a little shiny.

This will not help in giant, public pools. Unless you make your own tennis ball floaties (which you might want to do, just in case you are afflicted with a case of prose-inspired hypochondria).

Use 5: Remove Floor Scuff Marks

Any school janitor worth his salt knows that there's no need to scrub the floors like Cinderella just to remove some scuff marks. There's an easier way. A faster way. A better way.

In the irony of ironies, tennis balls remove scuff marks. I know! I'm sure you've been playing a match at the local courts and have seen the signs that say "No black-soled shoes." The signs are there to prevent the court from looking like a flat, green skate park, police academy driving range, or something else that is all scuffed up.[10] And to think,

---

[8]You could also make a dowel/tape/nail contraption to stick the string to the ceiling all in one go. Or just send a lanky friend onto the roof of your car. Or tie a string to a spear gun. There are other options, that's all I'm trying to say.
[9]Buttery people.
[10]Ran out of similes.

the tools to remove those scuff marks are *right there*.[11]

To remove those scuff marks, just put a tennis ball on a stick. Rubbed vigorously on top of a scuff mark, tennis balls act as an eraser. The felt has a good texture for removing the scuffs: rough without being too abrasive and gentle enough for special surfaces. Just like a school janitor.

Use 6: Massager

After a long day of pushing a giant rock up a hill, I imagine that Sisyphus gets tired. Maybe he could use a massage. But he's doomed to an

eternity of solitude. What's a lonely man to do if he needs some immediate relief in his sore muscles?

Grab a tennis ball, Sissy. Rub it over your boo-boo till it feels better. In fact, you can even lie down on that tennis ball to get a great back massage.

A tennis ball against the wall works for me. I just place it near the epicenter of pain, then wriggle around until it feels like I am no longer in jeopardy of suddenly separating into two halves like an earthworm. An earthworm with aspirational vertebral issues.[12]

(This also works on other muscle groups. It will not, however, work as a "personal" massager. Unless you are *way* into tennis.)

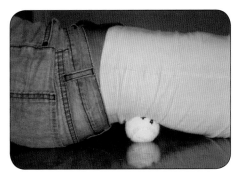

Use 7: Childproof Corners

There are few scenes scarier than seeing a child bleeding profusely from the face. Especially if that child is rapidly losing blood in *your* home.

If you're going to be hosting toddlers, or anyone else prone to running into sharp corners with the tender parts of their heads, try putting tennis balls over the nastier corners. If there's a bit of pipe jutting dangerously into your living space, pop a tennis ball

---

[11]Well, maybe. If any budding David Foster Wallace-types want to write up an explanation of the scuff-removal qualities of tennis balls, I'm sure we'd all appreciate it.
[12]Chordata ain't all it's cracked up to be, my little friend. Unless you have tennis balls.

on there. It'll deflect all but the most self-destructive of blows, and it'll give your home that "tennis pro" look that never goes out of style.

Use 8: Sand Curves

Under most circumstances, sanding is a necessary but unpleasant task. When you're sanding a curve that needs to stay curvy, try wrapping a tennis ball with sandpaper. It'll prevent the flat spots and unevenness that you might get if you only sanded by hand.

Pros can generally sand any shape without sanding down corners or otherwise permanently affecting the shape of their project. If you're failing to get a smoothly rounded shape, try a tennis ball.

Use 9: Jar Opener

Has this ever happened to you? You've just finished a particularly sweaty tennis match, and you reach into your bag for a delicious and refreshing jar of pickles. But the lid seems to be glued to the jar. Not even He-Man (nor the other masters of the universe) could get that thing open. No pickles for you!

Not so fast. A tennis ball cut in half can easily pop those lids off. Just cut along the seam of the tennis ball. That'll leave you with a bulbous little green friend, coated with rubber on the inside. You can get a great grip just by using the modded ball to get a handle on the lid.

Big thanks to **fungus amungus** for this awesome use of tennis balls.

Use 10: Photo Mount

Your pictures are probably wobbly. It's not your fault. You're a full-sized human being operating a camera the size of a pack of gum with a super-sensitive image sensor. If you breathe, you've ruined the shot. And you like breathing. So much so, in fact, that you will do it even while performing photography.

Like any good Instructaballer, you know that a tripod will make a world of difference. Perhaps you, like me, do not own a tripod. Perhaps you have a surplus of tennis balls. Perhaps you do have a tripod, but require a counterbalanced ball mount for steadiness off the 'pod.

Use 11: Put Stuff Inside

Tennis balls are hollow and easy to cut into. This makes them perfect vehicles for intra-office correspondence, hiding precious valuables at the gym, or any other activity that might require ballistic containment.

Just cut a slit into the side of the tennis ball. Cram in your message. Hurl it to your intended recipient. Or cut a slit into the side of the tennis ball. Cram in your cash. Stuff it under some dirty socks in your gym bag next to the Tinactin.

7 Unusual Uses for Barf Bags

By Wade Wilgus (wilgubeast)

(http://www.instructables.com/id/8-Unusual-Uses-for-Barf-Bags/)

Store Leftovers

Barf with Confidence on the Go

Hydrate

Throw Stuff Away Stink-Free

Airplane Puppets

Hold a Seat

Mailing Envelope

Worshipping at the porcelain altar. Shouting groceries. Shouting for Hugh. Calling Ralph on the big white telephone. Barf. Blow. Blow chunks. Hurl. Hork. Regurgitate. Lose lunch. Toilet tango. Spew. Puke. Gastrointestinal pyrotechnics. Upchuck. Yak. Airsickness. Carsickness. Seasickness.

Whatever you want to call it, barf bags will catch it. But they can do so much more. From airplane hacks to terrestrial, everyday uses, airsickness bags are more versatile than the world gives them credit for. And they're free.

Use 1: Store Leftovers

Not every restaurant provides bags, boxes, or other containers to safely bring home leftovers.

Airsickness bags are lined with plastic, have tabs to seal in the freshness, and fold nicely. You can surreptitiously stuff in all the bread you couldn't finish before the appetizers came. Or carry home the soup of the day. The same properties that hold in food post-digestion can also hold the same food prior to mastication.

Disclaimer: Using barf bags from the seat pocket on an airplane for food storage might be sort of gross. People do put their filthy tissues in there (among other things), and I can't imagine that those pockets get a thorough wash very often. It might be a little like eating off of a hotel bedspread. Your mileage may vary. I know a woman who swears by barf bags for storing leftovers and who has yet to get sick.

Use 2: Barf with Confidence on the Go

I have never done the Technicolor yawn on an airplane. I have, however, managed to woof my cookies in a number of other locations. As have many of you, I'd imagine.

An airsickness bag is a great accessory for pregnant women, college freshmen, and young schoolchildren. Anyone susceptible to vomiting while on the go could use an extra couple of bags. Keep them in your purse, in your backpack, or folded up in your back pocket behind your wallet. Never again will you be surprised by an encore performance of lunch, presented in reverse to everyone else on the bus.

It's the politest way to yak in public. They even sell cute ones.

Use 3: Hydrate

Getting enough water on an airplane is not easy. You can't bring liquids through security, bottled water is more expensive than gasoline once you're in the terminal, and the in-flight beverage service can maybe get you 8 oz. of liquid at a time.

If flying makes you desiccated and parched, you'll need to smuggle a water bottle on board. Empty. Or frozen if you're prepared to argue that the rules do not prevent you from bringing frozen solids aboard an aircraft.[13] Once you're aboard the plane, your liquid opportunities have pretty much dried up.

All hope is not lost. Using your airsickness bag as a funnel, you can get water from the lavatory to your water bottle. It's a little hack-y, but it works. You can also just fill the bag up then dump it into your water bottle. Because you won't have the necessary cutting implements to put a hole in the bag. It's better than waiting for the flight crew to wet your whistle.

Use 4: Throw Stuff Away Stink-Free

Sometimes you need to throw stuff away. Sometimes that stuff doesn't smell so awesome. Put the following things into a barf bag to seal in whatever scents you don't want wafting out of the trash can:

- Dog poop
- Old perfume
- Used feminine hygiene products
- Used male hygiene products
- Axe body spray
- Banana peels
- Burnt hair
- Chicken trimmings

There are more smelly things out there that fit inside a barf bag. This list is by no means comprehensive. But it should cover many cases.

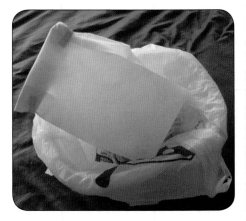

Use 5: Airplane Puppets

On the flight where I obtained my barf bags, a young mother was traveling with her eight-month-old child. No toys. No snacks. Just the natural beauty of mother and child together inside a big aluminum tube, just as Gaia intended.

That kid screamed and screamed.[14] Taxi, scream, take-off, scream, electronic devices back on, child still screaming. Which is understandable. If it was socially acceptable or even legal to articulate my feelings while in the airplane, I would

---

[13]The airport is a great place for lively scientific discussion. Argue with them about the possibility of electromagnetic interference causing plane crashes. Let them smell your water to prove it's safe. Explain that an e-ink screen is pretty much an Etch-a-Sketch when the wireless is turned off. Everybody loves learning. The more you know. . . .

[14]I was once a colicky baby who flew from Stapleton to JFK. Sorry, 1985 PanAm passengers. I get it. You and your baby need to go places. Airplanes are uncomfortable and upsetting. Babies aren't designed to seethe inwardly like the 6′5″ dude trying to simultaneously put his feet someplace and protect his elbows from the drinks cart.

likely yell right along with that small child's stentorian wails.

But I can't do that. Nor can I fire up anything to mitigate the din until we hit 10,000 feet. So please entertain your child. Try turning a barf bag into a puppet. Draw a face on with a pen. Make some funny voices. Everyone around you will appreciate the effort, even if it's unsuccessful. Anything's better than listening to your child scream past your increasingly frantic, embarrassed exhortations to please be quiet.

Use 6: Hold a Seat

Open seating on an airplane is a blessing and a curse. It's great when you want to save some cash, but the press of humanity struggling to get adjacent seats while avoiding weirdos and the middle seat can be unsettling.

Be one of those weirdos by using the barf bag early in the flight. Fill the bag up so it looks puffy and full. Set it on the seat you'd like to keep empty. Look ill. Point at the bag occasionally. Watch other passengers sit next to crying babies to avoid you.

This won't work on full flights, but it can be nice when there are thirteen open seats and you want to have elbow access to two armrests for the duration of your journey.

Use 7: Mailing Envelope

My dad is an envelope recycler. You know those windowed envelopes they stuff with junk mail addressed to "Your Name or current occupant"? He carefully opens them to get the free envelope. Write in the address to the right of the plastic window. Tape the whole thing shut.

For a similarly classy letter, with the added bonus of waterproofitude, use a barf bag. They're usually the right size for 4 × 6 pictures, you can affix labels and stamps to the outside, and the recipient will appreciate your creativity.

25 Unique Uses for Pantyhose

By Carley Jacobson (Carleyy)

(http://www.instructables.com/id/25-Unique-Uses-for-Pantyhose/)

Arm Tattoos

Photo—Gauze Lens

Polishing Cloths

Vacuum—Find Lost Objects

Pot and Dish Scrubber

Store Magazines

Ponytail Scrunchy

Cotton Ball Substitute—
Remove Nail Polish

Tie Objects Together

Duster

Stuffing

Test Sanded Surface for
Snags

Soap on a Rope

Patch a Hole in a Screen

Prevent Soil from Leaving Pot

Filtering Net

Food Strainer

Citrus Bath

Store Potpourri

Wash Cloth

Buff Your Shoes

Hang Onions

Cover a Bug Jar

Keep Warm

Clean Hairbrush

The life span of a daily-worn pair of pantyhose is *maybe* two months. I have actually had some pantyhose for years, but that's because I only wore them a couple times a year. So, let's say you get five good uses out of a pair of pantyhose—what else can you do with them?

I did a little research and found a bunch of ways to reuse your old, worn, lots 'o runs pantyhose.

Use 1: Arm Tattoos

I love this little trick. My friend was a basketball player for Halloween and wanted fake tattoos to complete her costume. She didn't want to draw on her arm, so she drew her designs on a pair of nude pantyhose and wore it on her arm.

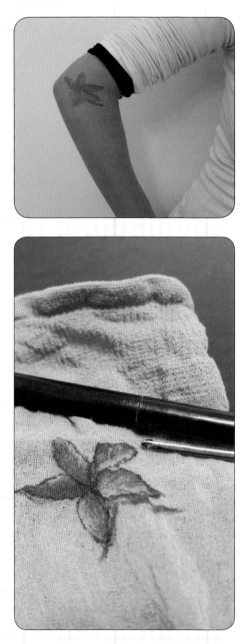

Use 2: Photo—Gauze Lens

Give your photos an eerie gauzy effect by covering the lens with your pantyhose.

Use 3: Polishing Cloths

Pantyhose are made of a soft, delicate material that makes them great for polishing most surfaces. I put the shine back in this old lamp just by giving it a light buffing. I didn't even use any polish—it's all in the pantyhose.

Use 4: Vacuum—Find Lost Objects

I am always dropping small objects like beads and the backs of my earrings on the floor. A simple way to find small lost objects is by placing pantyhose over the head of the vacuum hose, securing it with a rubber band (so the pantyhose

107

don't get sucked up!), and vacuuming under tables and chairs. The objects are quickly picked up without getting sucked away into the vacuum!

Use 5: Pot and Dish Scrubber

No need to keep buying new dish towels when you have *so* many old pantyhose. Clean cooked-on food and oil spills off your cookware. Just add dish soap and a bit of man power.

Use 6: Store Magazines

Tidy up your shelves and craft stations. You can use pantyhose to neatly store magazines and rolls of paper. The long thin shape of pantyhose is perfect for storing cylindrical objects. Just roll the magazines up and put them in the pantyhose, and they won't unravel.

You can see how neatly the magazines sit on the shelves above my washer and dryer.

Use 7: Ponytail Scrunchy

There's something about wearing pantyhose scrunchies that makes you want to take hundreds of Myspace photos in the bathroom. Check out a few of my favorite pics from my photo shoot.

How can you achieve this look? Cut off the top band of your pantyhose and tie it in your hair like a scrunchie.

Maximum adorability = SIDEPONY

Use 8: Cotton Ball Substitute—Remove Nail Polish

For some reason, I have always hated the way cotton balls feel. I can't really explain it, but squishing them makes me shudder. I usually use toilet paper when removing nail polish, but I found that using pantyhose is a much easier solution. Nail polish comes off faster and easier when you use pantyhose instead of cotton balls or toilet paper. You can also reuse the pantyhose, so no waste is produced!

Use 9: Tie Objects Together

Pantyhose have the amazing property of elasticity!

ELASTICITY, YOU SAY? But how can I utilize this elasticity?

Keep objects bundled together by tying a super stretchy pair of pantyhose around them!

Use 10: Duster

Dust your bookshelves easily and quickly. Cover your hand with a pair of pantyhose and just run it along a shelf, molding, or window sill.

Use 11: Stuffing

When dogs attack stuffed animals with their sharp teeth and cats maul your teddy bear's arm with their razor claws—perform some light surgery by replacing the stuffing with pantyhose.

WARNING: Never Google images of teddy bears in a place you don't feel comfortable ooh-ing and aww-ing out loud.

Use 12: Test Sanded Surface for Snags

Need to test your sanded surfaces for snags but scared of getting splinters? Try the pantyhose test. Put a piece of pantyhose around your hand and rub it over the wood. If the pantyhose snags onto any spots, you will know exactly where you need to re-sand.

Use 13: Soap on a Rope

. . . or in your old pantyhose. Same concept—different contraption.

Store old bits of soap in your pantyhose. Use it at the sink or in the shower to keep yourself clean. You can even use a new bar of soap for this. The pantyhose helps exfoliate your skin, so it's a two in one process!

Use 14: Patch a Hole in a Screen

For a temporary fix to a hole in your screen door, use pantyhose and duct tape to patch small areas.

Use 15: Prevent Soil from Leaving Pot

You don't want dirt and muddy water coming out of the bottom of your flower pots. You can prevent this by lining your flower pots with your old pantyhose.

Use 16: Filtering Net

Cut down the leg of your pantyhose so you have a flat piece of fabric. Cut out an even rectangle and tape it to a square frame. Use an old wire coat hanger for your frame.

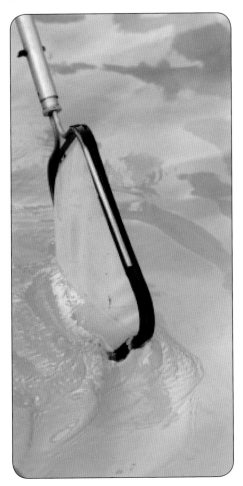

Use 17: Food Strainer

To prevent food from getting down your sink's drain, cover your bowl with a pair of pantyhose before pouring it in the sink. This is useful when you are having soup and you don't want to throw the liquid in the trash.

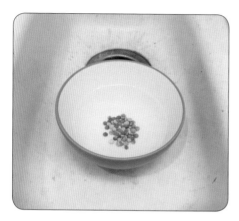

Use 18: Citrus Bath

Draw yourself a soothing citrus bath. It's simple: Grind up some lemon and orange peels and put them at the foot of your pantyhose. Tie a knot at the top and let it sit in the water.

Use 19: Store Potpourri

Fill the foot of your pantyhose with potpourri and hang in your closet. This will keep any small space from getting stinky!

Use 20: Wash Cloth

Exfoliate your skin by washing your face with a pair of old pantyhose. Pantyhose are perfect because they are gentle on your skin but they are rough enough to remove dead skin.

Warning: You will probably not want to use the foot section of your pantyhose, so be sure to cut it off.

Use 21: Buff Your Shoes

Refresh your worn out dirty shoes by giving them a good, fresh polish. Buff them with a medium-length strip of pantyhose. I refreshed my favorite pair of white patent leather pumps. I was able to easily remove small marks and bits of dirt. Unfortunately, years of wearing these shoes at frat parties in three-inch, beer-covered floors has left scuff marks that even a professional couldn't fix.

Use 22: Hang Onions

Use this quick fix for stopping onion and garlic skins from peeling off all over your counter. Put them in your pantyhose and let them hang from your cabinets. You still have easy access to them and you don't have to deal with the mess!

Use 23: Cover a Bug Jar

Kids love to bring strange creatures into the house. Whether it's a slug from the garden or a friend from class who likes to eat slugs, it's inevitable. When your kids come in the house with a hand full of bugs, put them in an old jar and cover it with a rubber band and pantyhose.

Use 24: Keep Warm

I used this trick all the time when I lived in upstate New York. It's easy to layer your shirts, but it's not so easy to layer your pants. In the winter, wear your old pantyhose under your pants for an extra layer of insulation. It doesn't matter how old and worn out your pantyhose are, because no one will see them!

Use 25: Clean Hairbrush

Stretch a small piece of pantyhose over your brush head. Use a bobby pin or pen to push it down below the bristles. When you are ready to clean the hair out of your brush, simply remove the pantyhose and throw it all out.

11 Unusual Uses for Diapers

By Wade Wilgus (wilgubeast)

(http://www.instructables.com/id/11-Unusual-Uses-for-Diapers/)

Mess-Free Flowers

Flame-Retardant Gel

Antiperspirant and Deodorant Wipes

Ultimate Paper Towels

Soil Conditioner

Fake Snow

Self-Inflating Flood Control Bags

Rescue Waterlogged Books

Ice Pack

Treat Equine Lameness

Pranks

Disposable diapers are a hotly-debated product among infants and toddlers alike. Some object to them on ecological grounds—throwing away all of those poop burritos wrapped in ultra-absorbent tortillas can't be good for the earth. Others laud them for their easy, no-mess design. Most just appreciate anything that doesn't leave a trail of feces down their legs.

Diapers (unused) are incredibly useful in non-baby applications. We're talking uses like:

- Fire and flood prevention
- Body odor mitigation
- Increasing crop yields
- Early fall skiing
- And so much more

Really, most of the uses are applications of the absorbent material in the diapers. But sodium polyacrylate isn't something you can just pick up down at the Piggly Wiggly. So we're talking about diapers. Disposable ones.

Read on for a hot, steaming load of knowledge.

Use 1: Mess-Free Flowers

Do you need to carry fresh flowers? Do they need to stay watered? Are you concerned about spillage during transport?

Pretty much every day.[15]

Sprinkle some sodium polyacrylate into the water holding your flowers to make a gel. Your flowers will still receive all that sweet, succulent moisture. Just without the mess. Or you could carry a bouquet in a diaper, but that kind of undermines whatever point you were trying to make by giving a special somebody those flowers.

Use 2: Flame-Retardant Gel

During a wildfire, some houses are covered in a flame-retardant gel made from the same stuff as disposable diapers. Flame-retardant gels are made from sodium polyacrylate that absorbs many hundreds of times its own weight in water. The gel is composed of a bunch of little bubbles that are filled with water and wrapped in a polymer shell. That shell forms a thermal barrier that requires more heat energy to destroy than normal foams that are composed of air bubbles.

You can make your own gel by removing the sodium polyacrylate from a disposable diaper. Fireproof small items in your home by dipping a diaper in some water then wrapping it around the object that needs protection.

Going on Pampers raids to find enough diapers to protect your entire house is impractical. You're better off following the local fire department's advice on clearing brush from the immediate vicinity of your home, but it's nice to know that you can keep your mint-condition action figures safe with a diaper if it comes down to it.

(Big thanks to **Goodhart** for providing the inspiration for this one.)

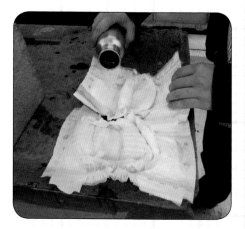

---

[15]Or just at prom, weddings, funerals, and the occasional day after a forgotten anniversary.

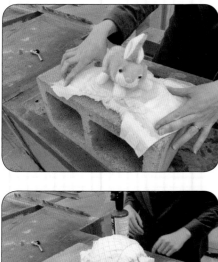

dampness. Whether at a job interview, on a first date, or reaching up for the handles on a bus, staying fresh is important. But it can be difficult. Once you've applied the antiperspirant/deodorant of your choice in the morning, that's it. Your armpit's destiny has been irrevocably established for the day. Or has it?

If you've got a diaper with you, you've got a chance to ameliorate any unanticipated perspiration. The absorbency of the sodium polyacrylate will slurp up whatever your sweat glands have decided to secrete. Some diapers are scented, so they'll even leave your pits smelling fresh as a baby's bottom.

So imagine this: You're riding the bus to a job interview with your first date. Your armpits are gushing like the opening sequence of the *Beverly Hillbillies*. You can feel the beads of sweat form on your skin and soak into your shirt. You discreetly remove a scented diaper from your bag, wipe down those pits with the chemical magic of the Dow corporation, and you're back in the game. Date went great, nailed the interview, and you didn't have to be the stinky person on the bus. All thanks to diapers.

Use 3: Antiperspirant and Deodorant Wipes

You're a big kid now. Look what you can do. You even wear big-kid pants.

The problems of youth are no more. You have new, big-kid problems. Like death, taxes, and extreme underarm[16]

---

[16]And other places.

Use 4: Ultimate Paper Towels

Bottom line, diapers are good at absorbing disconcerting volumes of filth. Next time you spill an entire bowl of cereal, milk and all, onto your travertine, try using a diaper to clean up the mess. You'll need to unfold it in such a way as to present the absorbent, sphincter-facing side of the diaper to the spill. Just perform a wipe/scoop with the diaper, then toss the whole mess into the garbage.

If you're on the go, use the hook and loop tabs on the side of the diaper to keep it sealed. Then you can carry your mess with you until you find an appropriate trash receptacle.

The sodium polyacrylate in the diaper is built to absorb liquids. In the diaper versus paper towels celebrity death match,[17] diapers are a clear favorite. They'll beat the pants clean off the competition. Just don't switch to diapers entirely—that might be rather cost-inefficient.

Use 5: Soil Conditioner

The one problem with the soil in your garden: It's not laced with super absorbent polymers that deliver more water to a plants' roots than normal soil.

Remedy that with a sprinkling of sodium polyacrylate. It's been scientifically proven (is there any other way?) to increase the biomass and yield of wheat plants.[18] Just keep everything from completely drying out or the soil conditioner could end up sucking water away from your plants.

To bring the power of your diapers to bear in the garden, cut open the diaper to get the sodium polyacrylate out. You can apply it directly to the soil, or, if you'd like to be more conservative, you can wrap the polymer in some cheese cloth to get the absorption effect without getting sodium polyacrylate all up in your dirt. Or just bury a wet diaper.

Use 6: Fake Snow

If you have a child who wears/wore disposable diapers, you probably dreaded accidentally allowing one of them into the laundry.[19] Washing a diaper produces some interesting results. Namely, a white slush of sodium polyacrylate spattered all over your freshly-laundered scivvies.

You can make productive use of the immersed sodium polyacrylate by making your own fake snow. Just add some water to the sodium polyacrylate. You probably won't get enough of a yield to practice taking on moguls (snow bumps, not Rupert Murdoch), but it makes a fun lab experiment when teaching/learning about polymers.

Just don't dump this slush down the drain, unless you want to explain how you gutted a diaper to make fake snow to a bemused plumber who will need to unclog your pipes. You won't be the

---

[17]Pampers Baby vs. Brawny Man.

[18]Presumably this should work with other plants as well. I see an elementary school science fair project in the making. . . .

[19]To eliminate this problem, run that load once more with salt instead of detergent. It'll disrupt the ionic balance and help you clean up without needing to pluck off each maggoty speck of damp diaper fluff.

person with the weirdest thing in their pipes, but you'll get mentioned to the plumber's loved ones over a meal at some point. There is no plumber-client privilege. To dispose of your fake snow, use the trash can. (Although I suspect with the proper chemical knowledge, you could fully disrupt the ionic bonds and chemically change the sodium polyacrylate into something that won't gum up the waterworks.)

footage of people frantically filling bags knows that it takes a *lot* of bags to divert an ornery torrent), so diapers might not be the best option when the Mighty Mississippi or Naughty Nile start overflowing their banks. But they might give you a bit of a head start if you are caught by surprise by the Perfect Storm and a nearby drainage ditch. Or a particularly splashy bath. Or an obnoxious neighbor who aims his downspouts at your basement.

Use 7: Self-Inflating Flood Control Bags

When a flood is imminent, people start shoveling sand into bags to build makeshift levees to keep the rising water at bay. Shoveling sand into a sack is hard work. And sand doesn't expand much as it absorbs water.

But toss some sodium polyacrylate into a sack and you've got a flat-packable, self-inflating flood control bag that requires only the flood water itself to expand to full, water-blocking size.

It'll take you a fair number of diapers to make even one sack (and anybody who has watched news

Use 8: Rescue Waterlogged Books

Oh, no! You borrowed *Pride and Prejudice* from a friend, lit some candles, drew yourself a bath, and promptly dropped the novel into your lavender-scented bathwater.

Book: ruined. Friendship: strained. Relaxing soak: suddenly stressful.

Unless you've got a diaper on hand, in which case, you can save two out of three. Just open the diaper up, insert it in between the dampened pages, and let the sodium polyacrylate slurp up your delicious autumn treat. Close the book around the diaper, prop the book up out of the sun, run a fan, and wait.

Some notes: If your book has glossy pages, you'll need to isolate each individual page to prevent making a brick of stuck-together pages. The National Archives and Records Administration Preservation Program says you have 48 hours to act to prevent mold and mildew. They also do not mention this trick. Which leads me to believe that it doesn't scale well, but it'll work for smaller spills.

Use 9: Ice Pack

A freezer bag. Some alcohol. Some water. And a diaper. Apart, they are merely a normal shopping trip. When combined, however, they form a Megazord of ice-packy goodness. Here's the basic premise:

- Dribble a cup of alcohol into the diaper.
- Then soak it in water.
- Bag it.
- Freeze it.
- Slap it onto an aching body part or into your lunch box.

The alcohol keeps the water from completely freezing. The sodium polyacrylate keeps the liquids suspended in a gel. And you're only out a diaper and a freezer bag. But you gain temporary relief from pain or warm beverages.

Use 10: Treat Equine Lameness

With horses, it's all fun and games until someone loses a hoof. If any of the horses in your life are suffering from a hoof abscess or other infection, you can use disposable diapers as part of a poultice to localize abscesses or draw out inflammation. Just use an over-the-counter hoof poultice or a DIY mix of wheat bran and Epsom salts, then wrap the hoof in diapers for a warm, moist environment without the deleterious effects of completely soaking the foot over time. Because constant immersion weakens the hoof walls, a disposable diaper makes an inexpensive and breathable bandage.

But don't take it from me. Here's what Stephen E. O'Grady, DVM, MRCVS, has to say about it: An ideal foot bandage is a medium-sized disposable diaper covering the enclosed medication. For more padding, use multiple diapers. For a sweating effect, use plastic-covered diapers and duct tape. For more breathing, use non-plastic covered diapers and gauze bandage. The bandaged foot is protected as well as medicated.

Your mileage (and horsepower) may vary.

Use 11: Pranks

The Crazy Diaper Prank from **Kipkay** is less useful but more amusing.

One prank involves microwaving a candy bar inside of a diaper, then eating the gooey mess publicly.

The other uses the sodium polyacrylate crystals (or pee pee crystals as Kipkay calls them) to solidify someone's water when they are not looking. It takes about twenty seconds to completely gel up. If you do this in a restaurant, let the wait staff know that they shouldn't toss the mess into a sink.

CONVERSION TABLES

One person's inch is another person's centimeter. Instructables projects come from all over the world, so here's a handy reference guide that will help keep your project on track.

Measurement								
	1 Millimeter	1 Centimeter	1 Meter	1 Inch	1 Foot	1 Yard	1 Mile	1 Kilometer
Millimeter	1	10	1,000	25.4	304.8	—	—	—
Centimeter	0.1	1	100	2.54	30.48	91.44	—	—
Meter	0.001	0.01	1	0.025	0.305	0.91	—	1,000
Inch	0.04	0.39	39.37	1	12	36	—	—
Foot	0.003	0.03	3.28	0.083	1	3	—	—
Yard	—	0.0109	1.09	0.28	033	1	—	—
Mile	—	—	—	—	—	—	1	0.62
Kilometer	—	—	1,000	—	—	—	1.609	1

Volume										
	1 Milliliter	1 Liter	1 Cubic Meter	1 Teaspoon	1 Tablespoon	1 Fluid Ounce	1 Cup	1 Pint	1 Quart	1 Gallon
Milliliter	1	1,000	—	4.9	14.8	29.6	—	—	—	—
Liter	0.001	1	1,000	0.005	0.015	0.03	0.24	0.47	0.95	3.79
Cubic Meter	—	0.001	1	—	—	—	—	—	—	0.004
Teaspoon	0.2	202.9	—	1	3	6	48	—	—	—
Tablespoon	0.068	67.6	—	0.33	1	2	16	32	—	—
Fluid Ounce	0.034	33.8	—	0.167	0.5	1	8	16	32	—
Cup	0.004	4.23	—	0.02	0.0625	0.125	1	2	4	16
Pint	0.002	2.11	—	0.01	0.03	0.06	05	1	2	8
Quart	0.001	1.06	—	0.005	0.016	0.03	0.25	.05	1	4
Gallon	—	0.26	264.17	0.001	0.004	0.008	0.0625	0.125	0.25	1

conversion tables

Mass and Weight						
	1 Gram	1 Kilogram	1 Metric Ton	1 Ounce	1 Pound	1 Short Ton
Gram	1	1,000	—	28.35	—	—
Kilogram	0.001	1	1,000	0.028	0.454	—
Metric Ton	—	0.001	1	—	—	0.907
Ounce	0.035	35.27	—	1	16	—
Pound	0.002	2.2	—	0.0625	1	2,000
Short Ton	—	0.001	1.1	—	—	1

Speed		
	1 Mile per hour	1 Kilometer per hour
Miles per hour	1	0.62
Kilometers per hour	1.61	1

Temperature		
	Fahrenheit (°F)	Celsius (°C)
Fahrenheit	—	(°C x 1.8) + 32
Celsius	(°F – 32) / 1.8	—

About the Authors

Carley Jacobson (Carleyy) is the partnership and contest manager at Instructables.com. She earned her degree in Computer Science and Visual Arts from Union College where she spent the better part of her time in the digital art lab building physical computing sculptures or in the sculpture lab welding steel and carving rocks. Her projects range from soft circuitry to carpentry to costumery. Her costumes are so good that she was mistaken for Lady Gaga by a semi-reputable Internet news site.

Gregg Horton (frenzy) is the QA Engineer for Instructables.com. When he's not deliberately breaking the website, he makes excellent contraptions. Twitter-enabled coffee pots, musical underpants, and improvised gas masks are just the tip of the iceberg. You should really have a look at his whole catalog of Instructables works - he has made many quirky and fun projects.

Mike Warren (mikeasaurus) is the Play editor at Instructables. Nearly an architect by training, he makes tasty, dangerous, and fun things... sometimes all at once! He destroyed a microwave to determine if it could be used to melt metal. (It worked. Mostly.) He has spray painted dinosaurs with a spray can he made himself, brewed a potent pot of coffee using energy drinks and other legal stimulants, and deconstructed a pair of high heels to add dinosaurs to them.

Sarah James (scoochmaroo) is the editor of many top ebooks and the Food & Living channels on Instructables.com. Previously, she was a tailor for American Conservatory Theatre, make-up artist for Blue Man Group, and starred in a national tour of an original play. Part time mathemagician, bespoke suit tailor, mask maker, and NYT crossword master, Sarah received her MFA in theatrical design and technology from UT-Austin. Her crazy projects include everything from tiny food on sticks to epic glowing costumes.

Wade Wilgus (wilgubeast) is a former Oakland middle school teacher whose projects range from useful classroom activities to gluing mustaches onto pistachios. He is the managing editor of Instructables, but spends the majority of his time figuring out ways to integrate meaningful research and hands-on learning in the classroom. He is always astounded by the creativity of his colleagues, and encourages everyone to check out Instructables to see their brilliant work.

also available

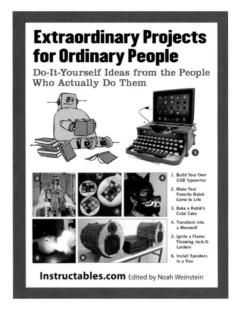

Collected in this volume is a best-of selection from Instructables, reproduced for the first time outside of the web format, retaining all of the charm and ingenuity that make Instructables such a popular destination for Internet users looking for new and fun projects designed by real people in an easy-to-digest way.

Hundreds of Instructables are included, ranging from practical projects like making a butcher block countertop or building solar panels to fun and unique ideas for realistic werewolf costumes or transportable camping hot tubs. The difficulty of the projects ranges from beginner on up, but all are guaranteed to raise a smile or a "Why didn't I think of that?"

Numerous full-color pictures accompany each project, detailing each step of the process along the way. It's an invitation to try a few yourself, and once you're done, see if you don't have a couple of ideas to share at Instructables.com.

US $16.95 paperback ISBN: 978-1-62087-057-0

also available

Continuing the Instructables series with Skyhorse Publishing, a mammoth collection of projects has been selected and curated for this special best-of volume of Instructables. The guides in this book cover the entire spectrum of possibilities that the popular website has to offer, showcasing how online communities can foster and nurture creativity.

From outdoor agricultural projects to finding new uses for traditional household objects, the beauty of Instructables lies in their ingenuity and their ability to find new ways of looking at the same thing. *How to Do Absolutely Everything* has that in spades; the possibilities are limitless, thanks to not only the selection of projects available here, but also the new ideas you'll build on after reading this book. Full-color photographs illustrate each project in intricate detail, providing images of both the individual steps of the process and the end product.

US $16.95 paperback ISBN: 978-1-62087-066-2

also available

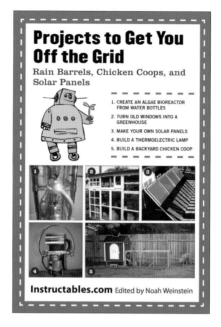

Projects to Get You Off the Grid

Rain Barrels, Chicken Coops, and Solar Panels

1. CREATE AN ALGAE BIOREACTOR FROM WATER BOTTLES
2. TURN OLD WINDOWS INTO A GREENHOUSE
3. MAKE YOUR OWN SOLAR PANELS
4. BUILD A THERMOELECTRIC LAMP
5. BUILD A BACKYARD CHICKEN COOP

Instructables.com Edited by Noah Weinstein

Instructables is back with this compact book focused on a series of projects designed to get you thinking creatively about thinking green. Twenty Instructables illustrate just how simple it can be to make your own backyard chicken coop, or turn a wine barrel into a rainwater collector.

Illustrated with dozens of full-color photographs per project accompanying easy-to-follow instructions, this Instructables collection utilizes the best that the online community has to offer, turning a far-reaching group of people into a mammoth database churning out ideas to make life better, easier, and in this case, greener, as this volume exemplifies.

US $14.95 paperback ISBN: 978-1-62087-164-5

notes

notes

notes

notes

notes